CITYSPOTS
LOS A

BEVERLY
HILLS

WHAT'S IN YOUR GUIDEBOOK?

Independent authors Impartial up-to-date information from our travel experts who meticulously source local knowledge.

Experience Thomas Cook's 165 years in the travel industry and guidebook publishing enriches every word with expertise you can trust.

Travel know-how Thomas Cook has thousands of staff working around the globe, all living and breathing travel.

Editors Travel-publishing professionals, pulling everything together to craft a perfect blend of words, pictures, maps and design.

You, the traveller We deliver a practical, no-nonsense approach to information, geared to how you really use it.

CITYSPOTS
LOS ANGELES

Written by Ryan Levitt
Updated by Tara de Lis

Published by Thomas Cook Publishing
A division of Thomas Cook Tour Operations Limited
Company registration No: 3772199 England
The Thomas Cook Business Park, 9 Coningsby Road
Peterborough PE3 8SB, United Kingdom
Email: books@thomascook.com, Tel: +44 (0)1733 416477
www.thomascookpublishing.com

Produced by The Content Works Ltd
Aston Court, Kingsmead Business Park, Frederick Place
High Wycombe, Bucks HP11 1LA
www.thecontentworks.com

Series design based on an original concept by Studio 183 Limited

ISBN: 978-1-84848-175-6

First edition © 2007 Thomas Cook Publishing
This second edition © 2009 Thomas Cook Publishing
Text © Thomas Cook Publishing
Maps © Thomas Cook Publishing/PCGraphics (UK) Limited
Transport map © Communicarta Limited

Series Editor: Lucy Armstrong
Production/DTP: Steven Collins

Printed and bound in Spain by GraphyCems

Cover photography (High rises and palm trees in LA) © Thomas Cook

CONTENTS

SYMBOLS KEY

The following symbols are used throughout this book:

ⓐ address ☏ telephone ⓦ website address ⓛ opening times
Ⓝ public transport connections ❶ important

The following symbols are used on the maps:

ℹ️	information office	🔲	points of interest
✈️	airport	O	city
➕	hospital	O	large town
Ⓒ	police station	○	small town
🚌	bus station	═	motorway
🚂	railway station	—	main road
Ⓜ️	metro	—	minor road
✝️	cathedral	—	railway
❶	numbers denote featured cafés & restaurants		

Hotels and restaurants are graded by approximate price as follows:
£ budget price ££ mid-range price £££ expensive

▶ Oscar statuettes

Introduction

The city of Los Angeles means so many things to so many people. It's the land of make-believe and glittering stars, a world of muscle cars and sun-bleached surfers, a place of amusement parks and musical piers. And it's also the location where so many dreams come true.

Southern California is like no other place in the United States, or, indeed, on the planet. A drive through Los Angeles can sometimes bring on a distinct feeling of déjà vu as familiar street names, chronicled in so many films, television shows and

○ *The legendary El Capitan Theatre on Hollywood Boulevard*

songs, flash by on every block. Your cultural frames of reference will be constantly a-jingle as you motorvate down the road. Is Sunset Boulevard a way of getting from Hollywood to West Hollywood? Or is it a metaphor for lost youth and glory? Or is it both? That's for you to decide.

Perhaps on account of the relative brevity of its history, Los Angeles has somehow found it necessary to create its own myths and legends. Its royalty is derived from the hierarchy of celebrity and its pageantry is displayed on screen, while its power brokers sit on their mobile phones closing six-picture deals. To see it in action is to see Hollywood at work. Who knows, while you're at dinner you might be witnessing the green-lighting of the next Best Picture winner at the very next table!

While travelling around the city is a challenge at the best of times, it's the addiction to car culture that makes LA unique. There's nothing quite like a drive through the Hollywood Hills, with the top of your convertible down and the wind rushing through your – preferably big – hair as you look down over the lights of the city, to make you feel you've stepped straight into the starring role in a movie.

Los Angeles adds wonder and magic to life. Whether in the form of a trip to Disneyland®, a tour behind the scenes at a film studio or a walk up Rodeo Drive, you're sure to be in awe of this place. New York may have the museums, Chicago the architecture, Miami the beach scene and Seattle the cool cafés – but Los Angeles has it all combined in one exciting and sun-drenched package. It's clear to see why this city means so many things to so many people – so why not come and find out what it means to you?

When to go

CLIMATE & SEASONS

Los Angeles has sunny, clear skies almost year-round. Rain is a rarity – but when it does come down, it comes down in buckets. The 'wet' months occur from January to March, although even during this time the average rainfall is a mere 9 cm (3½ in). Despite this, it has a strong effect as the arid soil quickly gets drenched and churns into mud. Landslides in the Hollywood Hills occur every year, destroying millions of dollars worth of property. Luckily, the owners of these properties are so wealthy, they hardly feel the financial pain.

Smog is a constant problem; however, it gets especially bad during the hot summer months and when the Santa Ana winds flare up in October and November. June is also hazy as foggy mist bathes the city in a gloomy atmosphere. Most locals agree that the best months weather-wise occur in spring and autumn, when the temperature isn't too steamy and the air quality clears up.

It's almost never cold in Southern California. While snow can sometimes fall on the scattered mountain ranges that surround the city, it rarely touches ground in Los Angeles proper. The average annual daytime temperature hovers between 20 and 30°C (68 and 86°F); however, the dry atmosphere can make it feel even hotter. In summer, things really heat up and measurements soaring above 40°C (104°F) are not unknown. The layer of smog over the city acts as a barrier that traps hot air beneath it, so when a heat wave hits, it stays.

If you need to cool yourself down, you'll find that the climate cools down the closer to the coast or the higher up the mountains you go.

○ *Angel or ghoul? You can't beat West Hollywood's Halloween celebrations*

ANNUAL EVENTS

The combination of a massive film industry and a vibrant collection of ethnic communities means that there is almost always a party going on in LA. A full calendar can be found on the Los Angeles Convention & Visitors Bureau website at Ⓦ http://discoverlosangeles.com

February
The Academy Awards The biggest show in town takes over every high-end hotel, restaurant, nightclub and venue in LA. Catch a glimpse of your favourite stars by camping out on the red carpet at the Kodak Theatre. For more details, see page 75. Ⓦ www.oscars.org

April
Fiesta Broadway The Latino community of the city celebrates Cinco de Mayo with one of the world's largest street parties. Join in the fun by heading Downtown. Be sure to practise your piñata-breaking skills in advance of the day. For more details on Cinco de Mayo, see page 14. Ⓦ www.fiestabroadway.la

July
Independence Day Los Angeles salutes the red, white and blue with a live performance at the Hollywood Bowl, featuring the LA Philharmonic Orchestra. Massive fireworks displays transform the night sky. Other great celebration spots include Disneyland®.
US Open of Surfing See the big boys ride the waves at America's largest surfing competition held on Huntington Beach. Live music,

food stands and unique boutiques line the beach, catering to the crowd of more than 200,000. ⓦ www.usopenofsurfing.com

October
West Hollywood Halloween Costume Carnaval West Hollywood puts on the best show of masked marauders, and daunting drag queens attempt to outscare each other. Head to Santa Monica Boulevard between Doheny and La Cienega to see the wildest of the bunch. ⓦ www.westhollywoodhalloween.com

November/December
Hollywood Christmas Parade More than a million fans line the streets of Hollywood to see this glittering parade of celebs and Santas. ⓦ http://cms.hollywoodsantaparade.com

PUBLIC HOLIDAYS
New Year's Day 1 Jan
Martin Luther King Jr. Day 3rd Mon in Jan
Presidents' Day 3rd Mon in Feb
Memorial Day Last Mon in May
Independence Day 4 July
Labor Day 1st Mon in Sept
Columbus Day 2nd Mon in Oct
Veterans Day 11 Nov
Thanksgiving Day 4th Thur in Nov
Christmas Day 25 Dec

Cinco de Mayo

On the last Sunday in April, the Latino community of Los Angeles comes alive to celebrate Cinco de Mayo – the day back in 1862 when Mexico defeated French invaders. You might think it a bit strange that Los Angeles would celebrate a Mexican holiday, but with such a large Mexican population calling LA home, it shouldn't come as too much of a surprise. In fact, the Cinco de Mayo celebrations in Los Angeles are the largest in the world.

The heart of the action is Downtown in the area surrounding Olvera Street. More than 500,000 revellers cover the 36 blocks of the Downtown core in a feast of food, live music and entertainment. Big-name Latin performers are a highlight of the day, with names such as Celia Cruz, Marc Anthony (Mr Jennifer Lopez) and Tito Puente having graced the stages during the event's history.

Many think Cinco de Mayo is Mexico's Independence Day, but this is a misconception. Mexico's independence actually came back in 1810 when the nation declared independence from Spain on 16 September. While this event is important in Mexican history, Cinco de Mayo is a fiesta that honours Mexican pride and is therefore a more popular event.

In fact, many attribute the Mexican success as a vital key in the win of the Union Army over the Confederates during the American Civil War. The French were decidedly pro-South. Had they succeeded in winning the battle over the Mexicans, they would have continued supplying the Confederate army with much-needed weapons and food – and the Civil War might have taken a different turn.

While many feel that LA's Cinco de Mayo celebrations have become over-commercialised, it shouldn't stop you from joining the throngs. It's an incredible way to expose yourself to Latin culture and the happiness is always effusive. For details, see Ⓦ www.fiestabroadway.la

◭ The colours and sounds of Mexico fill the air

History

Native Americans were in the Los Angeles area long before the arrival of Spanish missionaries in 1769. In order to colonise the region and convert the native population, settlements were established up and down the Californian coast.

The Mexican–American War of 1846–8 transferred to the Americans the California territory, then seen as an unruly region in the Wild West. Despite that fact, it took only a few short years before California joined the Union as the 31st state of America.

Los Angeles remained a backwater for almost the next 50 years until the arrival of the transcontinental highway linked the nation in 1886. As the population grew, demands on the scarce water resources increased and city engineers were forced to create massive dams and aqueducts to steer entire rivers towards the blossoming metropolis.

The massive expanses of cheap land and resources finally brought industry during the peak years of the 1920s as oil speculators and defence contractors moved in. Quickly following them were filmmakers who benefited from the large space and the golden light of California, which meant that longer filming hours could be arranged that wouldn't be affected by poor weather.

The Great Depression brought new strife to the city as poor farmers from the dust bowls of Texas and Oklahoma arrived, desperate to start new lives. Mexicans and African–Americans also began pouring in and colour wars started to rock poorer communities.

World War II affected many residents as the city's large Japanese population was forced into internment camps. Despite this, the city boomed as the defence factories went into overdrive. After the war, progress continued as freeways were built to reduce travel times and the threat of the Cold War kept the defence industry in business.

The 1960s saw severe class and race divisions increase. Affluent whites flocked from Downtown to the calmer neighbourhoods of the San Fernando Valley, away from the chaos of the big city. Racial tension continues to be the biggest challenge to the success of Los Angeles. Latinos now outnumber African-Americans as the largest minority by a wide margin in the city, as illegal migrants from south of the border melt into the population. Despite debates over immigration reform, many cite immigrants' contribution to the local economy as a good reason for preserving the status quo.

⬤ *Mary Pickford, one of Hollywood's earliest stars*

Lifestyle

Los Angeles is more than a city – it's a lifestyle. Certain things that you wouldn't even think of doing elsewhere are considered commonplace in this town and may cause you offence. Don't let them! Blending in will require you to shed some inhibitions, and create new ones. Americans are a very open people – especially Californians – so don't worry too much if communication wires get crossed.

An Angeleno will think nothing of starting a conversation with you, especially if they see you're a tourist. Unfortunately, the Angelenos who do this tend to be quirky, personality-wise. If you hate it when service people ask you if you need help or detest making small talk with strangers on a bus, you may have to adjust.

Americans love kitsch. A good example of this is the poster of the non-celebrity Angelyne, who is notable primarily for her large attributes and love of fuchsia bikinis. Despite the abundance of flesh on display, locals almost never talk about private sexual matters, and topless bathing on city beaches is absolutely forbidden. Prudishness runs deep in America, although a little less so in Los Angeles.

If someone appears to be talking to themselves, this doesn't necessarily mean they're having a psychological episode; they're just obeying the law and doing it hands-free. Multi-tasking is what it's all about. Making a call in the middle of dinner is not out of the ordinary, so don't be surprised if your dining companion has a 20-minute conversation while you sit opposite them – they might not see this as rude in the slightest.

And finally, a word on smoking. Due to the city's strict anti-smoking legislation, there is both good and bad news. The good news is you won't stink of smoke when you leave a club for the night and you can make fast friends with other smokers as you puff up in solidarity. The bad news is you will be a social pariah for the rest of the evening. For in Los Angeles, choking smog is fine, but carcinogenic smoke is not!

⬤ Look out for the likes of Jennifer Aniston at The Coffee Bean & Tea Leaf

Culture

Culture? In Los Angeles? Of course there is! While it might not be as visible or powerful as it is in New York or Chicago, there are still plenty of venues and galleries that would give even the Lincoln Center a run for its money.

The Downtown revival owes much to the artistic injection pumped into it by the arrival of the Walt Disney Concert Hall (see page 104) in 2003. This beautiful, large-scale venue, designed by local resident Frank Gehry, has been an architectural and

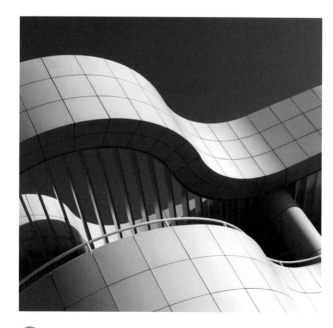

THE GETTY CENTER

It took over a decade – and $1 billion – for the Getty Center to finish construction, but what a result! Visitors will find this beautiful art museum difficult to get to due to limited public transport links; however, it's worth the extra effort if only to enjoy the spectacular views from its hillside setting.

Six pavilions house the permanent and temporary exhibitions, which, in turn, are surrounded by landscaped gardens and courtyards. But, it's the future potential of the museum that keeps the critics spellbound.

The current collection includes some fine examples from the Dutch Masters with modern photography and post-Impressionism also making a big impact. If you've been to the Met or the Louvre, you may find it all a bit ho-hum. The challenge the Getty faces is that, although it has plenty of cash to make purchases, it's playing a long game of catch-up in order to rival the great global galleries. It may be hard to afford a Van Gogh, but it's even harder to find someone who is selling one. However, they do boast more than 100,000 objects collected from the paintings, sculpture, drawings, manuscripts and photography disciplines. But ultimately, it's the architecture and sheer folly of the place that deserves recognition. ⓐ 1200 Getty Center Drive, Brentwood ⓣ (310) 440 7300 ⓦ www.getty.edu ⓒ 10.00–17.30 Tues–Fri & Sun, 10.00–21.00 Sat ⓝ Bus: 761

◀ *The spectacular Getty Center*

acoustic hit since the moment it opened its doors – and acts as the heart of LA's high-end cultural community. Now housing the LA Philharmonic, the Disney Hall adjoins three other venues: the Dorothy Chandler Pavilion (see page 102) (LA Opera), Mark Taper Forum (touring smaller musicals and plays) and Ahmanson Theater (Broadway hits and theatrical sensations). All three are housed at the Music Center (see page 104).

During the summer months, the Hollywood Bowl (see page 72) buzzes with outdoor activity. There's nothing better than enjoying a pre-show picnic or eating in your seats as you enjoy live classical, rock, folk or pop music under the evening stars.

Some of the biggest gems in Los Angeles are its art galleries. MOCA (see page 99), the Geffen Contemporary (see page 99) and the LA County Museum of Art (see page 65) are American highlights with plenty of big names. Just don't do as Steve Martin did in the film *LA Story* by donning roller skates to wander through the galleries. The security guards will quickly put an end to your 15 minutes reliving film fame.

▶ *Find your favourite stars in the Walk of Fame*

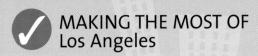

Shopping

Shopping isn't so much a pastime as a sport in Los Angeles. For many, shopping is their form of cardio, with entire days spent walking around malls and down exclusive streets in order to snag a bargain.

You can purchase pretty much whatever you might want in Los Angeles. Every big designer – American and European – has a boutique in this town, with Rodeo Drive in Beverly Hills and Melrose Avenue in West Hollywood holding the bulk of the big names. Speciality shops that offer lots of chic collections under one roof, such as Maxfield's and Fred Segal, are all the rage. Not so much department stores, they're more galleries for creative expression – only the art comes in the form of items you can wear. Make a beeline here if you want things like expensive one-off pairs of jeans, imported beauty products and accessories to die for.

Shopping centres are prevalent throughout the city, although there are decidedly more to choose from out in the suburbs, such as Pasadena and the San Fernando Valley. The Beverly Center is one of the most popular of the bunch, primarily due to its convenient location. You'll find most of the American big names such as Gap, Banana Republic and Victoria's Secret in these climate-controlled temples to capitalism.

For quirky, bohemian and unique offerings, West 3rd Street is a great area to explore. Independent bookstores, New Age emporia and original designers congregate here, all with an original outlook on life.

◔ Take the old-fashioned trolley to get around The Grove shopping centre

Food and drink fans should check out the Farmers' Market in the Fairfax District. This popular collection of organic food sellers and ethnic eateries is always a hit. And its location immediately next door to the popular outdoor shopping centre, The Grove, makes it a perfect one-stop shop. There's even a trolley ride through the middle of the mall, which younger children will adore.

Probably the most pleasant combination of mall and stroll is in Santa Monica on the 3rd Street Promenade. With street performers and cosy cafés hidden in the midst of all the national chains and one-off boutiques, you're sure to enjoy your time both in and out of the shops.

◆ *You'll find all the designers you can think of on Rodeo Drive*

Eating & drinking

Eating out is a way of life for most Angelenos. Depending on what you're doing and who you're doing it with, eating can be the finest of experiences or simply a quick bite en route along the freeway.

Studio apartment living *sans* kitchen is a common option for many residents. Who needs a cooker when you can 'order in' instead? Especially when you've got such an incredible array of delicacies to choose from. Local cuisine specialises in the flavours of its immigrants, a demand for healthy and fresh dishes or the finest in filling, fast food – but never all at the same time. Be sure to try a bit of everything before you board your plane bound for home.

Southern California is the land of the open road, bumper-to-bumper traffic and the terminus of thousands of cross-country car and truck journeys every year. Back in the 1950s, as automobiles became more accessible and highways opened up America, California responded by creating fast food. Fads such as drive-through diners and roller-skating waiters all started here, as chronicled in George Lucas' classic film, *American Graffiti*. Some of the best hamburgers, hot dogs and fried chicken can all be found in LA. Legendary one-offs and chains include Pink's hot

PRICE CATEGORIES
Average price for a main course.
£ up to $10 ££ $10–20 £££ over $20

dogs in Hollywood (where a queue is almost always guaranteed), Bob's Big Boy Burgers (considered the home of the artery-clogging, double-decker cheeseburger) and – of course – McDonald's.

Los Angeles' massive Latino community brings with it some of the best tastes in town. You'll never find better burritos, tacos or mole sauce than here. If you're looking for something authentic, and fast, then sit yourself down at any of the hundreds of taco stands dotted throughout the city. You'll find good, solid food

◐ Spago, Wolfgang Puck's flagship restaurant

catering to good, solid people at these shacks. They're a great place to meet and chat with locals originally from Latin America. There are even taco trucks that drive around town to cater for working crews and blue-collar workers. Find them located near construction sites and in industrial areas whenever you get a craving.

Olvera Street, while kitschy to say the least, is a great one-stop shop if you're looking to sample the flavours that come from 'south of the border'. Meals tend to be very filling, so be sure to arrive hungry.

Japanese cuisine is another must, especially sushi. There is a sushi bar on almost every street corner in town, and locals will always try to persuade you that their find should be your favourite. Going for sushi is a very local pastime. Much as other cities have a local curry house or Chinese takeaway, an Angeleno will think nothing of popping down for a quick California roll. As competition is so fierce, quality is extremely high. Only the freshest fish prepared by qualified chefs is used. Don't be surprised to find sushi and other Japanese dishes, such as tempura, served in shopping malls and at airport food courts.

Remember the scene in *Annie Hall* when Woody Allen goes to Los Angeles and orders a plate of mashed yeast? Well, the flavours of California have come a long way since then. Californian cuisine owes a great deal to Mediterranean kitchens, often featuring words like 'fresh' and 'organic' on the menu. Seafood is often highly featured and dishes will be light on sauces and focus more on the quality of the preparation. Some eateries even specialise in 'raw' food – dishes that are made completely out of uncooked vegetables in delicious combinations.

And the fact that you won't stink of cigarettes due to LA's strict anti-smoking laws means that both your lungs and your stomach remain happy and healthy.

🔺 *For fashionable fast food, try sushi*

Entertainment & nightlife

Work hard, play harder – that's the motto of Los Angeles. As the city is so spread out and residents are addicted to what's hip and hot, they think nothing of driving for miles in order to relax at a bar or club. Unfortunately, this means that drink-driving is rife, so be sure to have a designated driver or taxi number available before you set out for the evening.

As the home of Hollywood, maybe the obvious evening's entertainment is a trip to the cinema. For something a bit special, you might consider El Capitan (see page 72) on Hollywood Boulevard, which screens many film premieres. Mann's Chinese Theatre (see page 75), also on Hollywood Boulevard, similarly hosts major premieres.

While there are plenty of nightclubs, Los Angeles is primarily a live music venue. Everything from blues to jazz, and punk to funk can be seen in the halls and venues of this town. Competition is intense, so even if you aren't familiar with the acts, there's a good chance you'll walk away feeling as though you've just witnessed the next Red Hot Chili Peppers. For big names, the best venues are the **Nokia Theatre** (ⓐ 777 Chick Hearn Court ⓣ (213) 763 6030 ⓦ www.nokiatheatrelalive.com), the Staples Center (see page 36), **The Wiltern** (ⓐ 3790 Wilshire Boulevard ⓣ (213) 380 5005 ⓦ www.livenation.com/venue/the-wiltern) and the **Gibson Amphitheatre** (ⓐ Universal City Walk, 100 Universal City Plaza ⓣ (818) 622 4440 ⓦ www.hob.com). The Staples Center is where you'll find mega-name artists like Madonna, U2 and the Rolling Stones. With 20,000 seats to fill, a lot of pulling power is required. The sound quality here can be hit or miss, but you're

guaranteed a show you'll never forget. The Gibson is reserved for large (but not massive) R&B and pop bands. Think Pussycat Dolls or Jack Johnson for an idea of what to expect. Meanwhile, The Wiltern is the place of choice for rising stars and indie acts. This is the venue a lot of British acts play at when they first attempt to break the American scene.

Smaller names and emerging artists congregate around the Hollywood and West Hollywood scenes. Familiar venues like the legendary **Viper Room** (ⓐ 8852 W Sunset Boulevard ⓣ (310) 358 1880 ⓦ www.viperroom.com) and the even more legendary **Whisky A Go-Go** (ⓐ 8901 Sunset Boulevard ⓣ (310) 652 4202 ⓦ www.whiskyagogo.com), one-time stomping ground of such bands as the Doors and the Stooges, still draw the crowds. Check at the door or in advance to see what musical genre will be playing while you're in town.

For details on nightclub and live music performances, pick up a copy of the free *LA Weekly* listings guide, distributed in boxes around the city and in most hip neighbourhoods and bars.

◀ *Mann's Chinese Theatre hosts many major film premieres*

Sport & relaxation

PARTICIPATION SPORTS

The Pacific beaches provide ample opportunity for a spot of exercise, although weak swimmers may find the undertow a little challenging. If you are visiting with children, stick to beaches overseen by lifesaving units and keep watch over your little ones at all times. If you're an adventurous type, why not test your skills with a spot of surfing or boogie-boarding? There are plenty of surf shops up and down the coast where you can

● *The Dodger Stadium has been called the best baseball stadium*

rent supplies. Check surf conditions before you make the trek by calling the **Surf Hotline** (⊕ (310) 578 0478).

If you like a beachside location but don't want to get your feet wet, then the boardwalks are a great place to combine a spot of people-watching with jogging or rollerblading. You may have to jostle for position at weekends, when the volume of exercisers can become excessive.

Hikers will find plenty of challenging spots – all in incredibly inspiring environments. The Santa Monica Mountains, Hollywood Hills, Griffith Park and San Gabriel Mountains all offer amazing trails to tackle. Be sure to avoid a trip during the wet season as

THE STAPLES CENTER

As well as being a venue for rock concerts and trade fairs, the multi-faceted Staples Center is the home stadium of some of the city's leading sports teams. No fewer than three basketball outfits – the **Los Angeles Lakers** (ⓦ www.nba.com/lakers), the **Los Angeles Clippers** (ⓦ www.nba.com/clippers) and the **Los Angeles Sparks** (ⓦ www.wnba.com/sparks) – call the place home; meanwhile, ice hockey fans can enjoy the high-speed endeavours of the **Los Angeles Kings** (ⓦ http://kings.nhl.com). ⓐ 1111 S Figueroa Street ⓣ (213) 742 7340 ⓦ www.staplescenter.com ⓞ Box office: 09.00–18.00 Mon–Sat, 10.00–18.00 Sun ⓜ Metro: Pico

the paths can turn to mud, and sudden landslides can quickly put you in danger.

RELAXATION

Angelenos like to look good - because if you don't work in 'the industry', you at least have to look as if you do if you want any chance at a successful social life. Hitting the gym is considered part of everyday life in Los Angeles and is a fun way to chill out. Almost every hotel will have basic equipment, but **Gold's Gym** in Venice (ⓐ 360 Hampton Drive, Venice ⓣ (310) 392 6004 ⓦ www.goldsgym.com) is considered Mecca to muscular meatheads.

Accommodation

You get what you pay for in Los Angeles – and boy can you pay a lot. The city has everything from sleazy motels to famous 5-star hotels and everything in between. Some properties are as famous as the stars that frequent them, such as the Beverly Hills Hotel & Bungalows, the Mondrian, the Chateau Marmont and the Hotel Bel-Air. Others are popular due to their convenience and location.

A few years ago, low-service, high-design properties like The Standard became all the rage. But just as the celebrities come and go, so does the popularity of particular establishments. What's sizzle-hot one day may boast a graveyard of a lobby the next. Those on a budget should look into the possibility of hostels – although most guests are well under the age of 25. Be sure to keep your eye out for important conventions and awards ceremonies. When either (or both) are in town, rates can go sky high.

Hotels in the United States are graded according to a star system running from 1-star for a cheap guesthouse to 5-star for a luxurious property with numerous facilities.

HOTELS

Highland Gardens £ The interiors may be a little grim, but you can't beat the Hollywood location. The swimming pool adds a refreshing

PRICE CATEGORIES
All prices are for one night in a double or twin room.
£ up to $100   **££** $100–200   **£££** over $200

touch. ⓐ 7047 Franklin Avenue (Hollywood, West Hollywood & Fairfax) ⓣ (323) 850 0536 ⓦ www.highlandgardenshotel.com ⓝ Metro: Hollywood/Highland; Bus: 217

Farmer's Daughter ££ The actress Charlize Theron checked into this hotel for an extended period when she first hit town after emigrating from South Africa. A country feel is repeated throughout the property, giving it a warm touch. ⓐ 115 S Fairfax Avenue (Hollywood, West Hollywood & Fairfax) ⓣ (323) 937 3930 ⓦ www.farmersdaughterhotel.com ⓝ Bus: 217

Millennium Biltmore ££ If this hotel were located anywhere other than Downtown, it would be the most expensive in the city. Dripping with gilt, it's a stunningly opulent place to rest your head – and fantastic value for what you're getting. ⓐ 506 S Grand Avenue (Downtown) ⓣ (213) 624 1011 ⓦ www.thebiltmore.com ⓝ Metro: Pershing Square; Bus: 78, 79

The Standard Downtown ££ This hotel was the property that kickstarted the Downtown revival. DJs spin and swingers swig at this salute to the Jetsons era. ⓐ 550 S Flower Street (Downtown) ⓣ (213) 892 8080 ⓦ www.standardhotel.com ⓝ Metro: 7th Street; Bus: 760

Beverly Hills Hotel & Bungalows £££ The Pink Palace known as the Beverly Hills Hotel has been entertaining guests for almost a century. Elizabeth Taylor, Lana Turner and Marilyn

◗ *The Pink Palace, Hollywood's classic celebrity hideaway*

Monroe have all escaped the prying eye of the public at one time in the luxurious bungalows that sit away from the main building. ⓐ 9641 Sunset Boulevard (Hollywood, West Hollywood & Fairfax) ⓣ (310) 276 2251 ⓦ www.thebeverlyhillshotel.com ⓝ Bus: 2

Chateau Marmont £££ The Beverly Hills is to old Hollywood as the Chateau Marmont is to new. Leave the Pink Palace to the stars of yesteryear and mingle at this legendary hotel with rising rappers, comedians and – of course – ever present party girls Paris Hilton and Lindsay Lohan. ⓐ 8221 Sunset Boulevard (Hollywood, West Hollywood & Fairfax) ⓣ (323) 656 1010 ⓦ www.chateaumarmont.com ⓝ Bus: 2

Hotel Bel-Air £££ Owned by the Sultan of Brunei, this property is a favourite among royalty. Prince Charles is just one of the many famous guests who have checked in during the hotel's 80-plus year history. No two rooms are alike. ⓐ 701 Stone Canyon Road (Beverly Hills, Santa Monica & Venice) ⓣ (310) 472 1211 ⓦ www.hotelbelair.com

The Mondrian £££ Not as swanky as it used to be, the Mondrian still draws the crowds to the famous SkyBar (see page 71). Request a room away from Sunset Boulevard if noisy traffic bothers you. ⓐ 8440 W Sunset Boulevard (Hollywood, West Hollywood & Fairfax) ⓣ (323) 650 8999 ⓦ www.mondrianhotel.com ⓝ Bus: 2

Roosevelt Hotel £££ Once one of the ritziest hotels in town, the Roosevelt has been completely restored to its former glory.

The location in the heart of Hollywood is great for film fans. Interesting trivia: the first Academy Awards were held in the hotel ballroom back in 1929. ⓐ 7000 Hollywood Boulevard (Hollywood, West Hollywood & Fairfax) ⓣ (323) 466 7000 ⓦ www.hollywoodroosevelt.com ⓝ Metro: Hollywood/Highland; Bus: 217

HOSTELS

Banana Bungalow £ There's nothing quiet about this hostel, including the colour scheme. A riot of colour hits you as you enter the 'party dorm' atmosphere of this establishment. Choose to stay in a multi-bed dorm or book a private room. Some even have balconies. With a movie lounge and lively patio, you'll never be bored. ⓐ 603 N Fairfax Avenue (Hollywood, West Hollywood & Fairfax) ⓣ (323) 655 2002 ⓦ www.bananabungalow.com ⓝ Bus: 217

HI Santa Monica £ Spotless rooms in a fabulous location, just steps from the beach. All bathrooms are shared. Book well in advance as it is often full. ⓐ 1436 2nd Street (Beverly Hills, Santa Monica & Venice) ⓣ (310) 393 9913 ⓦ www.hilosangeles.org ⓝ Bus: 4, 704, SM1, SM7, SM8

THE BEST OF LOS ANGELES

Whether it's topping up your tan, spotting celebs, shopping till you drop or soaking up some high culture – there's something for everyone in Los Angeles.

TOP 10 ATTRACTIONS

- **Mann's Chinese Theatre** Inside and out, this theatre is one of the most amazing in the world. Be overawed by the architecture inspired by an actual Chinese temple or stay outside to find your favourite celeb caught in cement (see page 75)

- **Santa Monica Pier** Ride the Ferris wheel for a view over the Pacific that will inspire and delight (see page 80)

- **Disneyland®** The theme park that Walt built continues to captivate young and old alike (see page 110)

- **Rodeo Drive** Absolute excess Beverly Hills-style. Even if you can't afford a thing, the people-watching alone is enough to warrant a visit (see page 88)

Visitors gaze in awe at the set from Backdraft

- **Olvera Street** Authentically Mexican it isn't, but the sheer colour and vibrancy of this street should be enough to make you head Downtown (see page 96)

- **The Hollywood Sign** While you can't go near it, this sign has been a symbol of the city since it was erected in 1923. Thousands of stars and starlets have been beckoned by it ever since (see page 64)

- **Malibu** The perfect beachside community. See how many stars you can spot frolicking in the waves (see page 117)

- **The Academy Awards** The biggest night in Hollywood. It might be hard to find a hotel room, but the sheer glitter of the event should be enough to convince you (see page 66)

- **Museum of Contemporary Art** A gallery that takes post-war art to a new level – as only Los Angeles knows how (see page 99)

- **Paramount Studios** Still churning out the hits after all these years (see page 83)

Suggested itineraries

HALF-DAY: LOS ANGELES IN A HURRY

Go straight to Hollywood for a couple of hours dedicated to a bit of film history. Compare handprints at Mann's Chinese Theatre, spot the stars in the Hollywood Walk of Fame and then keep going until you catch a glimpse of the famous sign.

1 DAY: TIME TO SEE A LITTLE MORE

Explore Hollywood by day and then head over to Santa Monica for a bit of sun and sand. Ride the Ferris wheel at Santa Monica Pier and stroll through the shops on the 3rd Street Promenade.

2–3 DAYS: TIME TO SEE MUCH MORE

Spend a day at Disneyland® to get back in touch with your inner child, making sure to stop in Fantasyland to see Mickey himself. Follow this up with a day Downtown to see the heart of the city and its original settlement. Explore the ethnic neighbourhoods that dot the area and tuck into fresh sushi, chow mein or a beef burrito to savour the flavours of SoCal. Fit in a visit to the Watts Towers – Simon Rodia's amazing folk art constructions in LA's Watts District.

LONGER: ENJOYING LOS ANGELES TO THE FULL

Take a leisurely drive along the Pacific Coast Highway, making stops in Ojai, Malibu and Santa Barbara. Spend a day strolling up Rodeo Drive for a spot of window shopping, ending up at the Beverly Hills Hotel for a blow-out meal in the famous Polo Lounge. Tour a film studio and sit in the audience of an actual television taping. It's the perfect itinerary that combines surf, shopping, celluloid and sun in one amazing holiday.

◆ The Watts Towers – steel, concrete and glass folk art structures

Something for nothing

On a budget? Looking to fill some time? Well, there is no better option than a day at the beach. Los Angeles is Surf City USA and there are plenty of stretches of sand – each with its own distinct character to choose from.

Venice Beach is a world unto itself. Muscle-bound bodybuilders, botoxed beauties, rollerbladers and the alternative set all congregate here to show off their unique bodies and personalities. Don't be surprised if you see a grandmother in a bikini as she cycles down the boardwalk on a unicycle. That sort of vision is just the tip of the iceberg.

Further up the coast is Santa Monica. Families love the pier – and you don't need any money to stroll along its length. You will, however, have to fork out if you want to go on the rides or order something from the food stands.

Malibu, while a little way out of town, is the best place for surfing and bodyboarding. Zuma Beach is the place to go to enjoy the crashing waves. You'll find it located on the Pacific Coast Highway where the building numbers are in the 30,000s.

If sun, sand and surf don't appeal, you can always head over to Hollywood to compare your prints to those of your favourite stars in the pavement in front of Mann's Chinese Theatre (see page 75). See if you can spot where Humphrey Bogart, Cary Grant, Bette Davis, Harrison Ford, Tom Cruise and C3PO left their marks.

Finally, if you need a bit of culture in this city dedicated to the superficial, then the museums of Los Angeles make a great option. Many of the galleries are free of charge on certain days of the week or at specific times. The LA County Museum of Art (see page 65) is one possibility as it is free to enter every day of the week after 17.00 (barring Wednesdays, when it's closed). Other options include the La Brea Tar Pits (see page 65, free 1st Tues of every month) and the Japanese American National Museum (see page 98, free after 17.00 every Thur and free all day every 3rd Thur of the month).

● People-watching is fascinating on Venice Beach's Boardwalk

When it rains

It rarely rains in Los Angeles, but when it does, watch out! Sudden landslides can create havoc in the Hollywood Hills and Malibu, while traffic comes to a standstill as local drivers lack the skills to drive defensively in the challenging weather.

One of the best things to do when the heavens open is to go to the cinema. This is, after all, the town where most films are made – and where better to enjoy a flick than in Hollywood

⬤ *The Los Angeles County Museum of Art*

itself. Mann's Chinese Theatre is the best of the bunch; however, El Capitan is a close second. They're situated right across the street from each other, so if the feature in one doesn't appeal, you won't have far to go.

Visiting one of Los Angeles' museums is an excellent way to pass a wet morning. The Los Angeles County Museum of Art is home to plenty of big names (see page 65).

Live music is also an option, with clubs such as the Viper Room bringing hard rock, and venues like Disney Hall appealing to more classical tastes. The LA Philharmonic and LA Opera are both highly regarded; however, you might have trouble getting tickets on the day.

Angelenos love shopping and are masters at building shopping malls. Follow the sound of 'valley girls' as they smack their credit cards on the counter to any one of dozens of centres in the city. The Beverly Center is thought of as the best due to its range of shops and services and convenient access to Hollywood, Fairfax, West Hollywood and Beverly Hills.

Ever wondered how a TV show is made? Join the live studio audience of your favourite sitcom, game show or chat show by registering with **Audiences Unlimited, Inc.** (ⓣ (818) 753 3470 ⓦ www.audiencesunlimited.com) and choosing from dozens of daily tapings. Audiences Unlimited provides you with the keys to go backstage by taking part in an actual taping, although popular shows need to be booked well in advance. Recent shows have included *Two and a Half Men*, *America's Funniest Home Videos* and *Rules of Engagement*.

On arrival

TIME DIFFERENCE

Clocks in Los Angeles and Southern California follow Pacific Standard Time (PST). During Daylight Saving Time (early/mid-Mar–early Nov), the clocks are put forward one hour and Los Angeles adjusts to Pacific Daylight Time (PDT).

ARRIVING
By air

Travellers who fly to Los Angeles will most likely land at Los Angeles International Airport, otherwise known as LAX. Located in Westside, LAX boasts eight terminals; however, most arrivals from Europe land at the Tom Bradley International Terminal. The biggest exception to this rule is Virgin Atlantic, which lands at Terminal 2 of LAX.

From LAX, taxis to the Westside cost approximately $20–$25, to Downtown $42 and $55 to Hollywood and West Hollywood. A surcharge of $2.50 is placed on top of all taxis departing from LAX and you mustn't forget the standard tip of 10–15 per cent.

Less expensive options for those on a budget include the shared-ride **SuperShuttle** service (❶ 1 800 258 3826 ❷ www.supershuttle.com), starting at $25 per person, or the combined bus and subway service that goes as far as Hollywood. If you choose the latter, guard your luggage at all times and be sure to give yourself a minimum of two hours to reach your final destination.

Los Angeles International Airport (LAX) ❶ (310) 646 5252 ❷ www.lawa.org/lax

Aer Lingus ☎ 0870 876 5000 ⓦ www.flyaerlingus.com
Air Canada ☎ 0871 220 1111 ⓦ www.aircanada.com
Air New Zealand ☎ 0800 028 4149 ⓦ www.airnewzealand.co.uk
American Airlines ☎ 020 7365 0777 ⓦ www.americanairlines.co.uk
British Airways ☎ 0870 850 9850 ⓦ www.ba.com
Continental Airlines ☎ 0845 607 6760 ⓦ www.continental.com

🔺 *Union Station is a fine example of Spanish mission revival architecture*

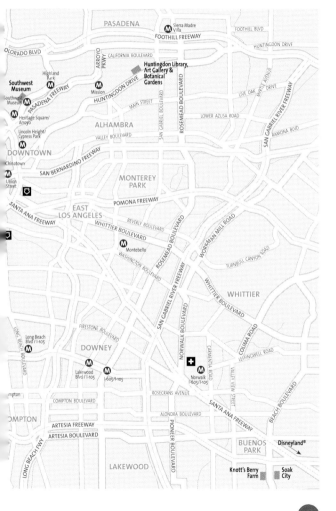

Delta ☎ 0845 600 0950 ⓦ www.delta.com
Lufthansa ☎ 0870 837 7747 ⓦ www.lufthansa.com
United ☎ 0845 844 4777 ⓦ www.unitedairlines.co.uk
US Airways ☎ 0845 600 3300 ⓦ www.usair.com
Virgin Atlantic ☎ 0870 380 2007 ⓦ www.virgin-atlantic.com

By rail

The main train station servicing Los Angeles is the Union Station in Downtown. Amtrak is the chief operator of passenger train services in America. Both cross-country and Pacific coast routes terminate here and connect with the Red and Gold lines on the subway system.

By road

While Los Angeles boasts an incredible network of highways, interstates and roads, the sheer volume of cars and collection of interchanges can sometimes boggle visitors. Once you get the hang of it, the city is extremely easy to drive through. Streets are wide and well signposted. Traffic is, however, packed at all hours of the day. If you are driving to Los Angeles, try to map your route out in advance in order to avoid confusion once you arrive within city limits.

FINDING YOUR FEET

The city centre of Los Angeles was once described by the author Dorothy Parker as '72 suburbs in search of a city'. With a description like that, you can imagine how big it is. Los Angeles itself is a conglomeration of the neighbourhoods that make up Los Angeles City and LA County. In addition, there are independent communities such as Beverly Hills and West Hollywood that sit somewhere in the middle of all of this. Confused? Don't be. Once you get the gist of things, Los Angeles is surprisingly easy to navigate - as long as you have a car.

ORIENTATION

Downtown is considered the heart (but not the most visited or picturesque neighbourhood) of Los Angeles, as it was here that the original Franciscan founders of the city created the Los Angeles pueblo settlement in 1781. Today it houses lofts, office buildings and hotels. Some blocks can be dangerous after dark and at weekends when city workers abandon the district.

Along the coast to the northwest are the Pacific Palisades and Malibu, while Venice and Marina Del Rey are southwest of Downtown. Santa Monica is right in the middle.

Culver City, WLA and Century City are west of Downtown, but not directly. From here, you can head north to Beverly Hills and West Hollywood. From West Hollywood, head east to central Hollywood and continue further east to Silver Lake. The Hollywood Hills separate Hollywood from the San Fernando Valley. To the west of the Hills is Brentwood and Bel-Air.

To the south of Downtown are the ethnically diverse communities of Watts and Compton. A wander through Watts with someone who knows the neighbourhood will showcase incredible soul food restaurants.

Further to the southeast is Anaheim – the land built by Disney and now featuring a plethora of exciting theme parks and family-focused adventures.

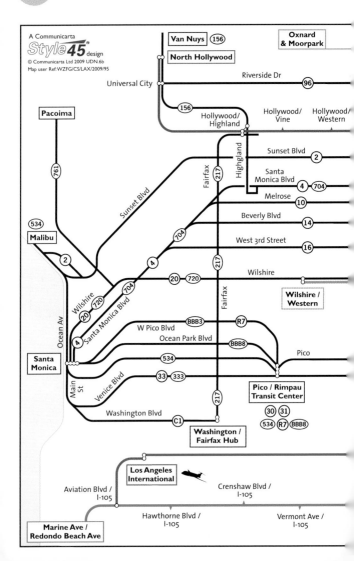

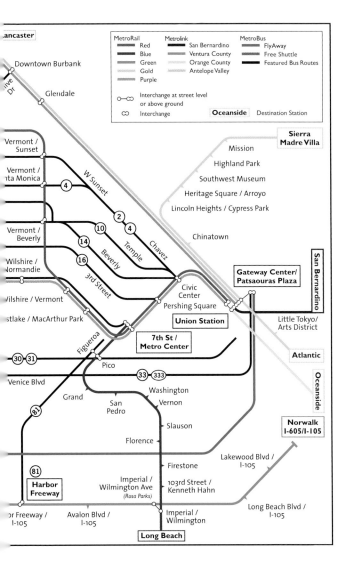

GETTING AROUND

Think twice before you plan a trip around Los Angeles by public transport. Most locals will think you are crazy to even attempt it. If you do, you are likely spend most of your day just getting to a single destination. That being said, there are several public transport options. **Metro** (w www.metro.net) runs five rail lines and well over 100 local and provincial bus lines. Santa Monica's **Big Blue Bus** (w www.bigbluebus.com) runs a bus service in and around Santa Monica. Big Blue Bus lines mentioned in this guide have an SM prefix to the relevant bus number.

CAR HIRE

You will need a car to see the sights of Los Angeles – and there are plenty of suppliers to choose from. Everything from tiny economy cars through to classic car convertibles is available, depending on your needs and sense of style. Petrol is much cheaper than in Europe, but a demand for big cars in America means you may be filling the tank more frequently. The minimum age for renting an economy car is 25 (or 21 if you are willing to pay a large surcharge). All the big names have a presence at the airport when you arrive.

Alamo ① (800) 462 5266 w www.goalamo.com
Avis ① (800) 230 4898 w www.avis.com
Budget ① (800) 527 0700 w www.budget.com
Hertz ① (800) 654 3131 w www.hertz.com
Thrifty ① (800) 847 4389 w www.thrifty.com

● *Los Angeles seen from Hollywood Hills*

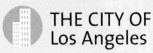

Hollywood, West Hollywood & Fairfax

Think of Los Angeles and the Hollywood sign is probably one of the first things that comes to mind. The tall letters overlooking this somewhat seedy, yet always glittering neighbourhood, have been beckoning starlets, movie stars and the tourists desperate to spot them, ever since they were erected back in 1923 as an advertising gimmick to draw potential buyers to a new housing district known as Hollywoodland. Numerous movie lots sprouted up in Hollywood during the early years of the 'silver screen', giving the area its celebrity-filled reputation. While the stars no longer call this area of LA home, there are still plenty of sights that hark back to the 'golden age of film' – and the district cashes in on its history at every opportunity. The Paramount Studios are the last remaining studios in Hollywood. For information on how

◆ There is no shortage of trendy diners when you need a break

to visit them – and all the other studios in Los Angeles – see the next chapter.

West Hollywood, meanwhile, is where today's stars party and play. Here is where you'll find the hottest clubs, the chicest hotels and top boutiques catering to the gay community and the enclave of B-list and television celebs, who mix and mingle with the masses.

For museums, culture, alternative shopping and a 'real people' vibe, head further south to the Fairfax District, where sights such as Melrose Avenue, the Los Angeles County Museum of Art, the La Brea Tar Pits and the popular Farmers' Market offer an injection of art into the local populace.

SIGHTS & ATTRACTIONS

Capitol Records Building

Several years on from its sale in 2006, a labyrinthine lawsuit means that the future of this Hollywood landmark remains uncertain. Built to resemble a stack of records complete with a stylus, it has seen thousands of recording artists walk through its doors since 1956. The actual building can't be entered so you'll have to admire it from outside. An interesting thing to note is that the blinking light at the top of the building spells 'Hollywood' in Morse code. ⓐ 1750 N Vine Street ⓝ Metro: Hollywood/Vine; Bus: 217

Hollywood Forever Cemetery

Probably the most visited cemetery in the world, after Paris' Père Lachaise, this cemetery is the final resting place for some of the

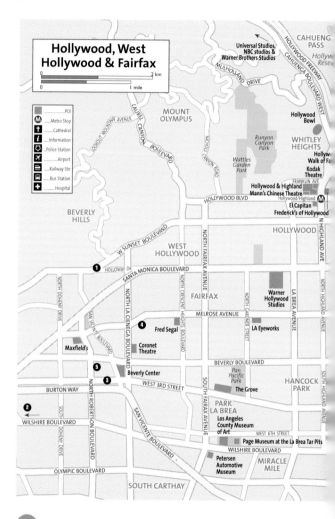

Hollywood, West Hollywood & Fairfax

0 ——————— 2 km
0 ——————— 1 mile

- POI
- Ⓜ Metro Stop
- ✝ Cathedral
- ℹ Information
- Ⓟ Police Station
- ✈ Airport
- 🚉 Railway Stn
- 🚌 Bus Station
- ✚ Hospital

Universal Studios,
NBC studios &
Warner Brothers Studios

CAHUENG
PASS

Hollyw
Rese

HOLLYWOOD FREEWAY

CAHUENGA BOULEVARD WEST

MULHOLLAND DRIVE

MOUNT
OLYMPUS

LAUREL CANYON BOULEVARD

LOOKOUT MOUNTAIN AVENUE

NICHOLS CANYON ROAD

Runyon
Canyon
Park

Hollywood
Bowl

WHITLEY
HEIGHTS

Hollyw
Walk of Fa

Wattles
Garden
Park

Kodak
Theatre

FRANKLIN AVE

Hollywood & Highland
Mann's Chinese Theatre

HOLLYWOOD BLVD

Hollywood/Highland Ⓜ

El Capitan

Frederick's of Hollywood

BEVERLY
HILLS

HOLLYWOOD

N HIGHLAND AVE

W SUNSET BOULEVARD

WEST
HOLLYWOOD

NORTH FAIRFAX AVENUE

① HOLLOWAY DR

SANTA MONICA BOULEVARD

NORTH DOHENY DRIVE

SAN VICENTE BOULEVARD

NORTH LA CIENEGA BOULEVARD

NORTH CRESCENT HEIGHTS BOULEVARD

FAIRFAX

Warner
Hollywood
Studios

LA BREA AVENUE

NORTH HIGHLAND AVENUE

MELROSE AVENUE

NORTH GARDNER STREET

④ Fred Segal

LA Eyeworks

Coronet
Theatre

Maxfield's

BEVERLY BOULEVARD

⑤

③ Beverly Center

WEST 3RD STREET

BURTON WAY

SOUTH FAIRFAX AVENUE

Pan
Pacific
Park

The Grove

HANCOCK
PARK

② ←

WILSHIRE BOULEVARD

SOUTH DOHENY DRIVE

NORTH ROBERTSON BOULEVARD

SAN VICENTE BOULEVARD

PARK
LA BREA

Los Angeles
County Museum
of Art

WEST 6TH STREET

Page Museum at the La Brea Tar Pits

WILSHIRE BOULEVARD

Petersen
Automotive
Museum

MIRACLE
MILE

SOUTH HIGHLAND AVENUE

OLYMPIC BOULEVARD

SOUTH CARTHAY

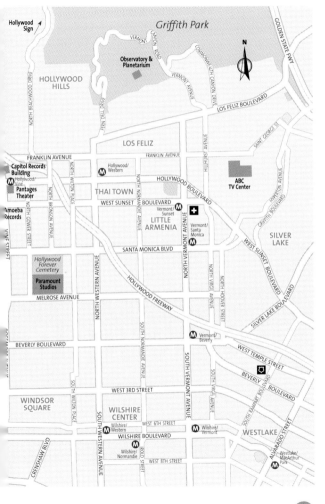

silver screen's greats, including Jayne Mansfield, Cecil B DeMille, Rudolph Valentino and Douglas Fairbanks. ⓐ 6000 Santa Monica Boulevard ⓣ (323) 469 1181 ⓦ www.forevernetwork.com ⓒ 08.00–17.00 winter; 08.00–18.00 summer ⓝ Bus: 4, 704

Hollywood Sign
Nestled in the Hollywood Hills, this symbol of the city has remained in the hearts – and eyes – of viewers since it was built to generate interest in the Hollywoodland real estate development. While it was only intended to stay for 18 months, locals fell in love with the 14 m (45 ft) tall letters and they were never removed. The sign seen today is actually the second

◐ *Don't miss Hollywood's iconic sign!*

set of letters built on the site following graffiti and arson damage caused during the 1970s. Security is tight, meaning that a close-up view is impossible. Further details can be found at ⓦ www.hollywoodsign.org

Hollywood Walk of Fame
More than 2,000 celebrities from the worlds of film, stage, television, music and radio are immortalised by the pink marble stars that line Hollywood Boulevard from La Brea Avenue to Gower Street. Some names you may have heard of, others might not be so familiar – but all catch your attention as you search for your favourites among the collection. Trivia fans should note that the first star was awarded to Joanne Woodward in 1960. Ⓜ Metro: Hollywood/Highland or Hollywood/Vine

CULTURE

Los Angeles County Museum of Art
LA gets a bad rap for culture; however, this glorious art museum does much to alter the situation. The collection boasts a vast array of American, African, European and Islamic art, including works by Degas, Gauguin, Toulouse-Lautrec and Hockney. A much-needed renovation will keep parts of the museum closed until late 2010.
ⓐ 5905 Wilshire Boulevard ⓣ (323) 857 6000 ⓦ www.lacma.org
ⓛ 12.00–20.00 Mon, Tues & Thur, 12.00–21.00 Fri, 11.00–20.00 Sat & Sun Ⓑ Bus: 20, 720. Admission charge (free after 17.00)

Page Museum at the La Brea Tar Pits
The nasty smell coming from a small section of Wilshire Boulevard

THE OSCARS

While the film industry dominates the city year-round, it doesn't show its full colours until the annual Academy Awards ceremony arrives at the Kodak Theatre in February. At this time of year, rooms in most hotels are at a premium, dinner reservations are impossible to come by and the population of Los Angeles is overcome with red carpets, stretch limos and waving celebs.

The Oscars are the crème de la crème of film awards. Legend has it that when the first awards were created, an employee of the Academy of Motion Picture Arts and Sciences (the organisation that dishes out the precious statues) remarked that the figure reminded her of her Uncle Oscar. The name has stuck ever since.

The lead-up to the Oscars is an exciting affair as the strip of Hollywood Boulevard between La Brea and Cahuenga is closed to traffic in order to prepare for the big event. Massive replicas of the famous statue depicting a knight holding a crusader's sword standing on a reel of film are erected along the street in addition to a massive red carpet that leads up to the Kodak Theatre where the event is held. Film fans have been known to camp out in the stands overlooking the entrance for up to a week in order to snag a prize spot close to their favourite stars.

For details on the Academy of Motion Pictures Arts and Sciences and the Oscars, visit Ⓦ www.oscars.org.

isn't LA's notorious smog – it's actually the odour of bubbling tar from the petroleum lake under Hancock Park. As far back as 1875, palaeontologists began digging fossils out of the asphalt in the area, and a museum was formed to showcase the more than 40,000 examples that have since been discovered. Next to the museum are the pits themselves, which continue to ooze much as they must have done millions of years ago. ⓐ 5801 Wilshire Boulevard ⓣ (323) 934 7243 ⓦ www.tarpits.org ⓛ 09.30–17.00 ⓝ Bus: 20, 720. Admission charge

Petersen Automotive Museum

In this city devoted to car culture, it makes sense that there is also a museum dedicated to covering its history and development. Little is provided in the way of explanation, but the sheer size of the collection never fails to impress. Everything from early automotive examples to models used in popular feature films is showcased. ⓐ 6060 Wilshire Boulevard ⓣ (323) 964 6315 ⓦ www.petersen.org ⓛ 10.00–18.00 Tues–Sun ⓝ Bus: 20, 720. Admission charge

RETAIL THERAPY

As distances are so far apart, street shopping can be a challenge. For chic boutiques, the shops of Melrose Avenue between Fairfax and San Vicente should be your first stop. Quirky choices and independent one-offs can also be found on West 3rd Street between La Cienega and Crescent Heights.

Fresh food and organic produce are the buy of choice at the popular Farmers' Market at Fairfax and West 3rd Street; however, it's the proliferation of shopping malls that truly provides the bulk of the buying options.

Amoeba Records This massive music store is the largest independent shop of its kind in the US. Both new and used CDs and DVDs are available. Staff are extremely knowledgeable, and very dedicated to keeping the shop unique when compared with its chain-store rivals. ⓐ 6400 W Sunset Boulevard ⓣ (323) 245 6400 ⓦ www.amoebamusic.com ⓛ 10.30–23.00 Mon–Sat, 11.00–21.00 Sun ⓝ Metro: Hollywood/Vine; Bus: 2

Beverly Center This mall has featured in dozens of films and television shows, so you may feel as if you've been here before you even step inside. All the usual suspects are available, including Macy's, Bloomingdale's and Gap. ⓐ 8500 Beverly Boulevard ⓣ (310) 854 0070 ⓦ www.beverlycenter.com ⓛ 10.00–21.00 Mon–Fri, 10.00–20.00 Sat, 11.00–18.00 Sun ⓝ Bus: 14, 16

Fred Segal A totally LA experience. Everything from local designers to American and street fashion big names under one roof. The biannual sales are legendary. Always a good place to spot a celeb. ⓐ 8100 Melrose Avenue ⓣ (323) 651 4129 ⓦ www.fredsegalbeauty.com ⓛ 10.00–19.00 Mon–Sat, 12.00–18.00 Sun ⓝ Bus: 10

Frederick's of Hollywood Truly trashy lingerie. The 'Fembot'-inspired negligees have to be seen to be believed. ⓐ 6751 Hollywood Boulevard ⓣ (323) 957 5953 ⓦ www.fredericks.com ⓛ 10.00–21.00 Mon–Sat, 11.00–19.00 Sun ⓝ Metro: Hollywood/Vine; Bus: 217

The Grove Small, open-air collection of mass-market shops and services including Abercrombie & Fitch and a popular multiplex. A small train running through the complex delights children. Adults arrive after shopping at the Farmers' Market next door. ⓐ 189 The Grove Drive, off Fairfax Avenue, next to the Farmers' Market ⓣ (323) 900 8080 ⓦ www.thegrovela.com ⓛ 10.00–21.00 Mon–Thur, 10.00–22.00 Fri & Sat, 11.00–19.00 Sun ⓝ Bus: 16, 217

Hollywood & Highland Tourist-focused shopping centre with a collection of names both unique and usual. Its location in the heart of Hollywood is its biggest draw. ⓐ 6801 Hollywood Boulevard ⓣ (323) 817 0220 ⓦ www.hollywoodandhighland.com ⓛ 10.00–22.00 Mon–Sat, 10.00–19.00 Sun ⓝ Metro: Hollywood/ Highland; Bus: 217

LA Eyeworks Ever wondered where Elton John gets his colourful specs? Well, wonder no longer. ⓐ 7407 Melrose Avenue ⓣ (323) 653 8255 ⓦ www.laeyeworks.com ⓛ 10.00–19.00 Mon–Sat ⓝ Bus: 10

TAKING A BREAK

The Coffee Bean & Tea Leaf £ ❶ Serving up the best coffee and ice-blended drinks in town, this celebrity favourite regularly sees such stars as Britney Spears, Meg Ryan and Jennifer Aniston queuing for a caffeine and sandwich fix. ⓐ 8789 W Sunset Boulevard ⓣ (310) 659 1890 ⓦ www.coffeebean.com ⓛ 06.00–00.00 Mon–Fri, 07.00–00.00 Sat & Sun ⓝ Bus: 2

AFTER DARK

RESTAURANTS

Mr. Chow ££–£££ ❷ Talk about celebrity central! Like the Ivy, this is another British import that has become a Los Angeles institution. Classic dishes like Peking duck are among the favourites, and garlic noodles are made in-house. ⓐ 344 N Camden Drive, off Wilshire Boulevard ❶ (310) 278-9911 ⓦ www.mrchow.com ⓛ 12.00–14.30, 18.00–23.30 Sun–Thur, 12.00–14.30, 18.00–23.45 Fri & Sat ⓝ Bus: 20, 720

Orso ££–£££ ❸ Sometimes the easiest way to describe an LA eatery is to name the celebs that frequent the place. Drawn to the immaculate Californian and Mediterranean cuisine on the menu are such luminaries as Sean Bean and Faye Dunaway. Big-time agents consider this place a fave. ⓐ 8706 West 3rd Street ❶ (310) 274 7144 ⓛ 11.45–22.00 Mon–Thur, 11.45–23.00 Fri, 17.00–23.00 Sat, 17.00–22.00 Sun ⓝ Bus: 16

Ago £££ ❹ Robert De Niro searched in vain for high-quality Italian cuisine in Los Angeles, so he invested in this eatery popular with big names such as Julia Roberts and Gwyneth Paltrow. The wine list is incredibly well stocked. ⓐ 8478 Melrose Avenue ❶ (323) 655 6333 ⓦ www.agorestaurant.com ⓛ 12.00–14.30, 18.00–23.30 ⓝ Bus: 10

The Ivy £££ ❺ Just like its British counterpart, you'll need a lot of clout to even snag a table at this ultimate celebrity hangout. The likes of Brad Pitt and Bill Clinton are regulars. Dishes are light, yet tasty. Service is hit and miss. 113 N Robertson Boulevard (310) 274 8303 11.30–22.00 Mon–Thur, 11.30–22.15 Fri–Sun Bus: 14, 16

BARS & CLUBS

The Bar So cool it doesn't even have a name, this drinking spot is certainly one of the hippest place in town among the music set. Dress to impress in your trendiest T-shirt and jeans. 5851 W Sunset Boulevard (323) 468 9154 http://thebarhollywood.com 21.00–02.00 Bus: 2

Bardot A gorgeously decorated party palace that pays homage to the Art Deco era of the building that houses it via regular burlesque shows; but there are disco nights, too. Once the home of infamous celebrity haunt, the Spider Club, the owners remodelled the sexy space in 2008, and now Bardot's is a great place for schmoozing and boozing. A limited menu is available. 1737 Vine Street (323) 462 8900 www.bardothollywood.com 20.30–02.00 Metro: Hollywood/Vine; bus: 217

Rage West Hollywood rivals San Francisco as the gay capital of the West Coast. A stop inside this always-packed establishment will convince you of this fact every night of the week. Club nights vary, but the crowd is always up for having a good time. 8911 Santa Monica Boulevard (310) 652 7055 www.ragewesthollywood.com 11.30–02.00 Bus: 4, 704

SkyBar It's not as hard to get in as it used to be, but this always-chic bar remains a great celeb-spotting venue. If you can't afford a room at the Mondrian Hotel, where the bar is located, then a drink here is the next best thing. Mondrian Hotel, 8440 W Sunset Boulevard (213) 848 6025 www.mondrianhotel.com 18.00–02.00 Bus: 2

The Viper Room No longer owned by Johnny Depp, this venue isn't as hip as it used to be. Its fame comes due to its notoriety as the location where rising star River Phoenix died. Punk bands of varying quality are the usual performers of choice. 8852 W Sunset Boulevard (310) 358 1880 www.viperroom.com Various Bus: 2

CINEMAS & THEATRES

El Capitan A grand dame of a cinema. Its purchase by Disney means that it's often the locale of choice for the studio's cartoons and film premieres. 6925 Hollywood Boulevard (323) 467 7674 http://disney.go.com/disneypictures/el_capitan Hours vary according to film schedules Metro: Hollywood/Highland; Bus: 217

Hollywood Bowl This massive outdoor amphitheatre has been hosting concerts since it was built in its spectacular Hollywood hillside setting back in 1921. Everyone who is anyone has performed here – from The Beatles to Monty Python. 2301 N Highland Avenue (323) 850 2000 www.hollywoodbowl.com 12.00–18.00 Tues–Sun, May–Sept (on show nights, the closing time is 30 minutes after the performance ends) Bus: 156

⬤ *A band performs at the popular Viper Room*

Kodak Theatre Major Broadway musicals and visiting companies make this theatre home, but it's the Academy Award ceremonies that are held here every February that have made the venue famous. Half-hour tours are available between 10.30 and 14.30. ⓐ 6801 Hollywood Boulevard ⓣ (323) 308 6363 ⓦ www.kodaktheatre.com ⓛ Hours vary according to performance schedules ⓝ Metro: Hollywood/Highland; Bus: 217. Admission charge

Mann's Chinese Theatre This cinema is famous for its collection of hand and footprints in the cement outside its front entrance. You can compare your feet to such luminaries as Marilyn Monroe and Judy Garland. ⓐ 6925 Hollywood Boulevard ⓣ (323) 464 8111 ⓦ www.manntheatres.com ⓝ Metro: Hollywood/Highland; Bus: 217

Pantages Theater This art deco masterpiece is a venue for major plays, musicals and performances. ⓐ 6233 Hollywood Boulevard ⓣ (323) 468 1770 ⓦ www.broadwayla.org ⓛ Vary according to performance schedules ⓝ Metro: Hollywood/Vine; Bus: 217

◀ *The Kodak Theatre is home to the Academy Awards ceremony*

Beverly Hills, Santa Monica & Venice

Long synonymous with West Coast wealth and sophistication, Beverly Hills is the place where the stars live out their daily lives. Rodeo Drive, with its high-end designer boutiques, acts as the unofficial 'Main Street' of the neighbourhood. And a stroll along its stretch is considered a must-do by both residents and visitors alike. Just try not to gawk at the botoxed beauties, accessorised puppies and plastic Paris Hilton look-alikes as they get out of their convertibles and Hummers.

Santa Monica is the beachside community of choice for upwardly mobile types and features a gorgeous boardwalk complete with a funfair on a pier.

Finally there is Venice Beach, named due to the collection of canals built to resemble the Italian city of the same name. LA's alternative community calls this neighbourhood home – and the sights of the famous Muscle Beach, pierced and tattooed residents and bikini-clad rollerbladers will be sure to make your jaw drop more than just a few times.

SIGHTS & ATTRACTIONS

Muscle Beach

This tiny corner of Venice's boardwalk is considered a Mecca for bodybuilding enthusiasts around the world. Arnold Schwarzenegger holed up here for much of the 1970s in order to show off his biceps to an adoring public. ⓐ Venice City Beach ⓝ Bus: 33

⬥ You can't beat Venice Beach for entertaining eccentrics

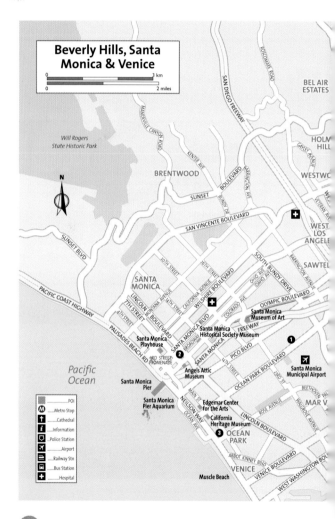

Beverly Hills, Santa Monica & Venice

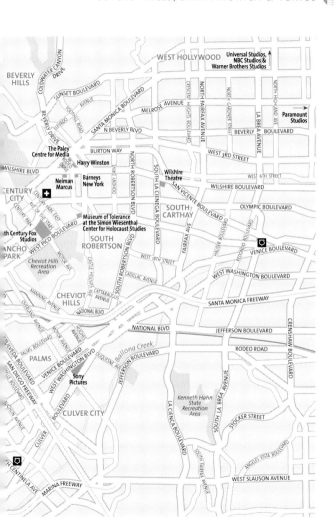

Santa Monica Pier

If you've ever been to Brighton or Blackpool, then you'll know what to expect here. The giant Ferris wheel on Santa Monica Pier provides breathtaking views over the ocean and seaside community, while more adrenalin and speed-focused rides lie at its base. A perfect place to bring kids in need of distraction. The whole place has a delightfully 'Americana' feel. Be sure to dig in to a ball of candy floss. ⓐ 200 Santa Monica Pier ⓣ (310) 458 8900 ⓦ www.santamonicapier.org ⓛ The pier itself is open 24/7; each business and ride has its own hours, and they vary by season ⓝ Bus: 33, 333, SM7, SM8

Santa Monica Pier Aquarium

It's not one of the best aquariums in the country, but it's a good place to bring children, and it makes a nice break from the decidedly more raucous offerings on the pier itself. ⓐ 1600 Ocean Front Walk ⓣ (310) 393 6149 ⓦ www.healthebay.org ⓛ 14.00–17.00 Tues–Fri, 12.30–17.00 Sat & Sun ⓝ Bus: 33, 333, SM7, SM8

CULTURE

Angels Attic Museum

Kids and adults alike love this quaint museum that displays more than 60 antique dolls' houses in minute detail. ⓐ 516 Colorado Avenue ⓣ (310) 394 8331 ⓦ www.angelsattic.com ⓛ 12.00–16.00 Thur–Sat ⓝ Bus: 4, 704. Admission charge

---

● *Affluent homes on Santa Monica beach*

California Heritage Museum

This museum is actually a restored house dating back to the late 19th century. Each room is devoted to a different period of Californian history and decorated to convey the look and feel of the time. Temporary exhibits add a touch of perspective to the decorative arts on display. ⓐ 2612 Main Street ⓣ (310) 392 8537 ⓦ www.californiaheritagemuseum.org ⓛ 11.00–16.00 Wed–Sun ⓝ Bus: 33, 333, SM8. Admission charge

Museum of Tolerance at the Simon Wiesenthal Center for Holocaust Studies

This gripping museum opened in 1993 to great acclaim. Combining film, displays, photographs and artefacts, the collection attempts to enlighten visitors about the causes and effects of the Holocaust and the immigrant experience. ⓐ 9786 W Pico Boulevard ⓣ (310) 553 8403 ⓦ www.wiesenthal.com ⓛ 11.00–18.30 Mon–Thur, 11.00–15.00 Fri, 11.30–19.30 Sun ⓝ Bus: SM7. Admission charge

The Paley Center for Media

A museum holding a vast collection of more than 100,000 TV clips that can be viewed by the general public. Look out for the regular talks and screenings given by some of the biggest names in the business. ⓐ 465 N Beverly Drive ⓣ (310) 786 1091 ⓦ www.paleycenter.org ⓛ 12.00–17.00 Wed–Sun ⓝ Bus: 4, 14, 704

Santa Monica Historical Society Museum

The history of the beachside community is told through photographs and newspaper headlines in this small museum whose move to the Santa Monica Public Library is due to be completed by early 2010.

Santa Monica Museum of Art

This delightful art museum, housed in a former trolley station, is devoted to the works of local and international up-and-coming artists. Exhibits can be eclectic but always entertain. ⓐ Building G1, Bergamot Station, 2525 Michigan Avenue, off Cloverfield Boulevard, which is off Olympic Boulevard ⓣ (310) 586 6488 ⓦ www.smmoa.org ⓛ 11.00–18.00 Tues–Fri, 11.00–20.00 Sat ⓝ Bus: SM7

STUDIOS

NBC Studios

While the NBC Studios tour may feel a little less 'starry' due to its focus on television, it remains a big draw, especially now that the best of US TV is reckoned to be superior to the country's cinematic output. The tour lasts about 70 minutes and is good value for money. Reservations aren't required, so a last-minute visit is possible. ⓐ 3000 W Alameda Avenue, Burbank ⓣ (818) 840 3537 ⓦ www.studioaudiences.com ⓛ 09.00–15.00 ⓝ Bus: 96. Admission charge

Paramount Studios

The Paramount Studios are the last remaining studios in Hollywood. The famous gates are a landmark in the city and feature fine examples of filigree ironwork – added when crazed female fans kept climbing over the original gates in order to meet their idol, Rudolph Valentino. The actual lot is massive and

TOURING THE STUDIOS

The original film studios were drawn to Hollywood due to the almost permanent dry conditions, golden sun and large plots of cheap land. Skyrocketing land prices and smog have since moved or shut down most of the lots, but there are still plenty of opportunities to see where and how the movie magic is made.

holds a working population of 5,000. A water tower looms over the entire complex, harking back to the days when the property had its own hospital and fire department. Reservations are essential. ⓐ 5555 Melrose Avenue, Hollywood ⓣ (323) 956 1777 ⓦ www.paramount.com ⓛ 10.00, 11.00, 13.00 & 14.00 Mon–Fri ⓝ Bus: 10 ⓘ Guests must be at least 12 years old. Admission charge

Sony Pictures

Simple walking tours for film and TV buffs. You must be over 12 years old to take part, and reservations are strongly recommended. ⓐ 10202 W Washington Boulevard, Culver City ⓣ (310) 244 8687 ⓦ www.sonypicturesstudios.com ⓛ 09.30, 10.30, 13.30, 14.30 Mon–Fri ⓝ Bus: C1. Admission charge

Universal Studios

For most, the biggest studio draw is Universal Studios – however, it is far from the most authentic of experiences. Universal Studios focuses more on rides and attractions than the actual art of film. Despite this, it's still a fun place to pass an afternoon. The studio tour itself is primarily staged and packed with scenes that will help you relive the excitement of past Universal hits including *Jaws* and *Earthquake*. An open-sided train whizzes you around the lot as a chirpy host reveals a few basic facts and figures about some of the films that have been shot on site. ⓐ 100 Universal City Plaza, Universal City ⓣ (800) 864 8377 ⓦ www.universalstudios.com ⓒ 10.00–17.00 Mon–Fri, 10.00–19.00 Sat, 10.00–18.00 Sun ⓝ Metro: Universal City; Bus: 96, 150, 240. Admission charge

🔺 *The famous gates of Paramount Pictures*

Warner Brothers Studios

True film buffs should head straight to these studios and book onto an exclusive deluxe tour. It may be expensive, but this five-hour tour goes further behind the scenes than any other studio tour in the city. This is probably the only tour where you might get a chance to spot stars and actual filming. ⓐ 3400 Riverside Drive, Burbank ⓣ (818) 972 8687 ⓦ www.wbsf.com ⓛ 08.20–16.00 Mon–Fri ⓝ Bus: 96. Admission charge

RETAIL THERAPY

3rd Street Promenade It's hard to know whether to describe this pedestrianised road as a street or a shopping mall. The shopping area runs between Wilshire Boulevard and Colorado Avenue, anchored at one end by a three-storey centre with all the big names in place such as Banana Republic and Gap. The street itself boasts even more shops, and makes for a pleasant change from the air conditioning on days when the call of the sun gets too much. ⓐ 3rd Street between Colorado and Wilshire ⓝ Bus: 4, 704, SM1, SM2, SM3, SM4

Barneys New York This branch of the famous New York department store is the shop of choice for those looking for designer jeans and fashionable casual wear and couture. ⓐ 9570 Wilshire Boulevard ⓣ (310) 276 4400 ⓦ www.barneys.com ⓛ 10.00–19.00 Mon–Wed, Fri & Sat, 10.00–20.00 Thur, 12.00–18.00 Sun ⓝ Bus: 20, 720

Harry Winston "Talk to me Harry Winston". That's what Marilyn Monroe cooed in her signature song 'Diamonds are a Girl's Best

⬥ *Rodeo Drive, home of expensive shopping*

Friend'. This renowned jeweller is the boutique of choice during the Academy Awards as they loan out millions of dollars worth of jewels to nominees and presenters every year. A walk by the window will dazzle you – so be sure to wear your shades! ⓐ 310 N Rodeo Drive ⓣ (310) 271 8554 ⓦ www.harrywinston.com ⓛ 10.00–18.00 Mon–Fri, 11.00–18.00 Sat ⓝ Bus: 20, 720

Neiman Marcus Top quality designer clothes and furnishings. But you pay for what you get. The range is impressive, but so are the price tags. ⓐ 9700 Wilshire Boulevard ⓣ (310) 550 5900 ⓦ www.neimanmarcus.com ⓛ 10.00–18.00 Fri–Wed, 10.00–20.00 Thur ⓝ Bus: 20, 720

Rodeo Drive Made famous in such films as *Pretty Woman* and *Clueless*, the main drag of Beverly Hills is a salute to capitalism. Big names such as Cartier, Ralph Lauren and Gucci line the immaculate street as celebrities, oil tycoons and trophy wives dot in and out of their doors. You might need a mortgage to afford to shop, but the entertainment in the form of the people-watching comes completely free of charge. Keep between Wilshire and Elevado for the bulk of the action. ⓝ Bus: 4, 14, 20, 720

TAKING A BREAK

Counter £ ❶ There's no country that does hamburgers quite like the United States. This great burger bar allows you (and your kids) to make your own, topping it off with more condiments and additions than you could ever imagine. The selection of cheeses alone should be enough to convince you. ⓐ 2901 Ocean

Park Boulevard ❶ (310) 399 8383 Ⓦ www.thecounterburger.com
🕐 11.00–22.00 Mon–Thur, 11.00–23.00 Sat, 11.30–21.00 Sun
Ⓝ Bus: SM8

AFTER DARK

RESTAURANTS

Juliano's Raw £ ❷ The raw food fad started here at this
vegetarian eatery that dishes up the finest organic courses
around. Choose from vegan sushi, Mexican burritos and pizzas,
all featuring raw vegetables combined in delicious combinations.
ⓐ 609 Broadway ❶ (310) 587 1552 Ⓦ www.planetraw.com
🕐 10.00–22.00 Sun–Thur, 10.00–23.00 Fri & Sat Ⓝ Bus: SM7, SM8

Sushi Roku ££ ❸ There are literally thousands of sushi joints
in Los Angeles, and this is one of the better ones – in terms
of interiors and sophistication, that is. Far from authentic,
Sushi Roku draws the hipsters of the city due to its minimalist
look and feel and fusion-style offerings. East meets West in
a great combination. ⓐ 1401 Ocean Avenue ❶ (310) 458 4771
Ⓦ www.sushiroku.com 🕐 11.30–14.30, 17.00–23.30 Mon–Fri,
12.00–23.30 Sat, 16.30–22.30 Sun Ⓝ Bus: 4, 33, 704, 534, SM7, SM8

BARS & CLUBS

Avalon Hotel Lounge Housed in the lobby and around the
kidney-shaped swimming pool of a retro hotel, this popular
martini and lounge bar is a hit with wealthy movers and
shakers. ⓐ 9400 Olympic Boulevard ❶ (310) 277 5221
Ⓦ www.avalonbeverlyhills.com 🕐 06.00–00.00 Ⓝ Bus: 14, 28, 728

Bar Pintxo Run by well respected local chef Joe Miller and inspired by the tapas bars of Spain, this cosy eatery offers many a delectable nibble – not least at the bar – and an impressive selection of some two-dozen wines by the glass. But the great thing about Pinxto is its atmosphere: it sets out to be your home-from-home local and all but the terminally churlish would deny that it achieves its ambition. Indeed, the inclusive, welcoming vibe and retinue of hardy regulars evokes a distinctly Mediterranean feel. ⓐ 109 Santa Monica Boulevard ⓣ (310) 458 2012 ⓦ www.barpintxo.com ⓛ 10.00–00.00 Tues–Thur, 12.00–00.00 Fri–Wed ⓝ Bus: 4, 704

Chez Jay Casually eclectic, this laid-back bar has been a Santa Monica institution for more than 40 years. A great place if you're wanting to kick back without all the door policies and snobbery associated with other LA drinking holes. ⓐ 1657 Ocean Avenue ⓣ (310) 395 1741 ⓦ www.chezjays.com ⓛ 17.30–22.00 Mon, 11.30–14.00, 17.30–22.00 Tues–Sun ⓝ Bus: 333, SM7, SM8

Otheroom This microbrewery boasts one of the widest selections of beer, ale and lager in the city. ⓐ 1201 Abbot Kinney Boulevard ⓣ (310) 396 6230 ⓦ www.theotheroom.com ⓛ 17.00–02.00 ⓝ Bus: 33, 333

CINEMAS & THEATRES
Santa Monica Playhouse This respected live theatre venue draws big names to its season of classics. Two stages offer a complete season of works. ⓐ 1211 4th Street ⓣ (310) 394 9779 ⓦ www.santamonicaplayhouse.com ⓛ Varies ⓝ Bus: 20, 720

EDGEMAR CENTER FOR THE ARTS

This area's proximity to Hollywood casts rather a strange complexion on the local performing arts scene: those with a thick enough skin to go for it among the super-competitive wannabes find it inspirational; those who want to express themselves artistically but don't necessarily spend the hours between waiting-job shifts refining their Oscar acceptance speech can find it intimidating. Locally, the Edgemar is known as probably the one place whose rehearsal areas really do see rampant egos sweating happily alongside the violets who might elsewhere cringe. Indeed, its emphasis on collaboration as opposed to competition has made this Frank Gehry-designed performing arts centre the most significant player on the local scene. Its sometimes breathtakingly good productions take place in two theatre spaces, and there are smaller areas for comedy, music and dance. ⊕ 2437 Main Street ⊕ (310) 399 3666 ⊕ www.edgemarcenter.org ⊕ Box office: 09.00–18.00 Mon–Fri ⊕ Bus: 333, SM8

Wilshire Theater Multi-purpose venue that sees both live theatre and hip bands perform on its stage. The art deco interiors give the place an intimate feel. ⊕ 8440 Wilshire Boulevard ⊕ (323) 655 0111 ⊕ www.wtbh.org ⊕ Box office: 12.00–18.00 Tues–Sat ⊕ Bus: 20, 720

Downtown

By day, Downtown bustles with lawyers, accountants and civil servants. By night, the district is transformed into the city's trendiest new neighbourhood. Up until a few years ago no one entered the area's streets after dark or at weekends, when LA's homeless community moved in. Now, with developments such as the Walt Disney Concert Hall and the chic Standard Hotel bringing money into the community, safety levels are improving.

Downtown is also well known for its exciting ethnic communities. Chinatown is headquartered in these parts, as is the city's vibrant Mexican community (around Olvera Street). Little Tokyo – a region named for its large Japanese community – is also centred here.

SIGHTS & ATTRACTIONS

Chinatown

A large Chinese population has existed in Los Angeles since the mid-19th century. The focal point for the neighbourhood is a bizarre shopping centre called Central Plaza. Here you will find the bulk of Chinese New Year celebrations and shops selling Chinese herbs, trinkets and delicacies. The food is far from authentic but it's a friendly part of town with plenty of hole-in-the-wall bars to pass the time in. ⓐ Main roads: N Broadway and N Spring Street Ⓜ Metro: Chinatown; Bus: 45, 83, 84

El Pueblo de Los Angeles Historical Monument & Olvera Street

This pleasant monument was created to honour the original

⬥ *The gates of Chinatown*

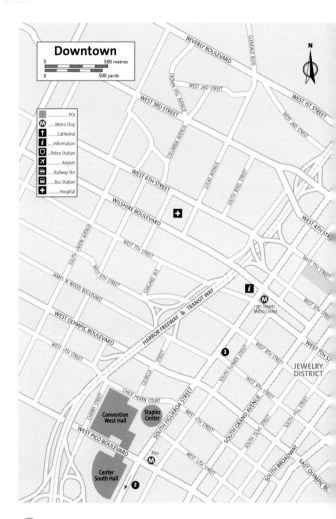

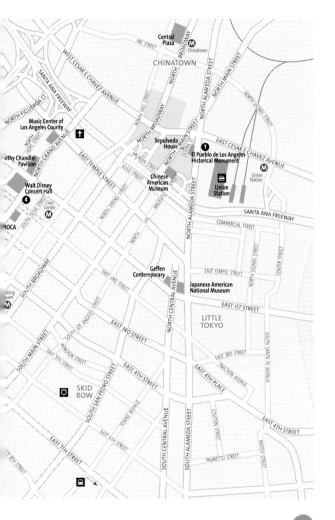

settlement that brought the first residents of Los Angeles to the region. On the site is a collection of buildings dating back to the late 19th and early 20th centuries, with the pedestrianised Olvera Street running alongside the home of the centre's museum, Sepulveda House.

Olvera Street is dedicated to LA's vast Mexican community, offering up a jumble of eateries, souvenir stands and clothing sellers. Be sure to keep a look out for the Avila Adobe nearby, which is the city's oldest house, built in 1818.

Sepulveda House acts as the visitor's centre for the area, chronicling the history of the early settlement. It's worth a stop inside if you are interested in the region's proud Latino past.

Go to the southern end of Olvera Street to enjoy the live Mexican music performances regularly scheduled in the bandstand at the centre of the public plaza.

Sepulveda House ⓐ 622 N Main Street ⓣ (213) 628 1274 ⓦ www.cityofla.org ⓛ 10.00–15.00 Tues–Sat ⓝ Metro: Union Station

Union Station

The city's Union Station is one of America's last rail palaces built during the days when train travel was the fastest and most glamorous way to cross the country. It's a temple to Spanish colonial and mission revival and is one of the finest architectural examples of the period in the Western United States. Even if you aren't boarding, it's worth a look. ⓐ 800 N Alameda Street ⓝ Metro: Union Station

---

ⓞ *Go to Olvera Street for live music*

CULTURE

Chinese American Museum

Exhibits documenting the city's Chinese population provide the lifeblood of this museum, which also acts as a Chinese-American community centre. 🅰 425 N Los Angeles Street 🅘 (213) 485 8567 🅦 www.camla.org 🕐 10.00–15.00 Tues–Sat 🅜 Metro: Union Station. Admission charge

Japanese American National Museum

Following the Chinese Exclusion Act, which barred Chinese from emigrating to the United States in 1882, the Japanese began moving in to take their place. They began their lives working in extremely hard conditions as cheap farm labour and continued to pour in to grasp their slice of the American Dream until a series of new laws in 1913 prevented them from owning land. The

▲ The Downtown skyline

internment camps of World War II created even more hardships. It wasn't until 1952 that people born in Japan were actually permitted to become US citizens.

The museum itself is top-notch, telling the story of the Japanese-American experience. Both permanent and temporary exhibits are on display, in addition to the collection of the National Center for the Preservation of Democracy, which serves to promote the ideals of democracy in the United States. ⓐ 369 East 1st Street ⓘ (213) 625 0414 ⓦ www.janm.org ⓛ 10.00–17.00 Tues & Wed, Fri–Sun, 12.00–20.00 Thur ⓝ Bus: 30, 31. Admission charge (free after 17.00 every Thur and free all day every 3rd Thur of the month)

Museum of Contemporary Art & Geffen Contemporary

Two museums in one! Local darling, Frank Gehry, designed the Geffen – widely considered to be the finest in the West for post-war art (but please note that it is closed for renovation until November 2009). Close by is the larger MOCA, linked artistically, but not physically, to the Geffen itself. The permanent exhibition includes works from Rothko, Mondrian and Pollock, but it's the temporary collections that bring in the big names. As many as 12 revolving shows can be seen at one time, with MOCA focusing on conservative artists and Geffen pushing the envelope.

MOCA ⓐ 250 S Grand Avenue ⓘ (213) 621 2766 ⓦ www.moca.org ⓛ 11.00–17.00 Mon & Fri, 11.00–20.00 Thur, 11.00–18.00 Sat & Sun ⓝ Metro: Civic Center; Bus: 2, 4, 10, 14. Admission charge

Geffen Contemporary ⓐ 152 N Central Avenue ⓘ (213) 621 2766 ⓦ www.moca.org ⓛ 11.00–17.00 Mon & Fri, 11.00–20.00 Thur, 11.00–18.00 Sat & Sun ⓝ Bus: 30, 31. Admission charge (free 17.00–20.00 Thur)

> ### SKID ROW
> While Downtown is changing, there are still pockets that should be avoided, and LA's Skid Row at 5th Street between Main and Alameda is one of them. Long the destination of choice for the city's homeless, it's a dangerous street and home to drug dealers, abandoned psychiatric patients and recently released convicts. Stay as far away as possible unless you want to become another statistic.

RETAIL THERAPY

Broadway For a taste of true Mexican culture, head to Broadway. Once home to the city's entertainment district, you'll still find a few reminders of this period in the form of the former Million Dollar Theater, located at No 307. This is where the legendary Sid Grauman began his empire, which culminated in the construction of Mann's Chinese Theatre in Hollywood (see page 75). Other theatres include the Orpheum, the Pantages and the United Artists Theatre. Also located here is the Bradbury Building, a masterpiece in 20th-century architecture that is most famous for having been used as the location in the filming of the penultimate scene of *Blade Runner*.

But it's the shopping that truly gives this street its flavour. As the city's Latino community becomes more affluent, it flexes its dollars. A combination of both bargain basement boutiques and increasingly expensive offerings are available – with more exclusive options opening every day. ❷ S Broadway between

East 1st Street and West 7th Street ⊚ Metro: Civic Center/ Pershing Square

Jewelry district Shop for gems and anything else that glitters in this bustling part of town. You'll need to know what you're doing if you want to find a bargain. ⊜ Hill Street and Broadway between 6th and 8th Streets ⊚ Metro: 7th Street/Metro Center

TAKING A BREAK

Philippe the Original £ ❶ This diner invented the original French Dip, a delicious sandwich of carved meats on a soft bun dipped in the meat's juices. Lunchtimes are packed with local workers, so be sure to get in early. ⊜ 1001 N Alameda Street ⊕ (213) 628 3781 ⊚ www.philippes.com ⊕ 06.00–22.00 ⊚ Metro: Union Station

AFTER DARK

RESTAURANTS

Chano's £ ❷ For melt-in-your-mouth burritos, you can't go wrong with the selection at this stand. Go hungry, as your stomach will be full by the time you take your last bite. Definitely not for dieters. ⊜ 3000 S Figueroa Street ⊕ (213) 747 3944 ⊕ 08.00–01.00 Sun, 08.00–02.00 Mon–Wed, 08.00–03.00 Thur–Sat ⊚ Bus: 37, 38

Original Pantry £ ❸ The true greasy spoon experience in the heart of LA. Open 24 hours, it draws a large crowd eager to soak in the authentic diner atmosphere and the grease on the plates of fries, burgers and hearty home cooking. ⓐ 877 S Figueroa Street ⓣ (213) 972 9279 ⓦ www.pantrycafe.com ⓛ 24 hours ⓝ Metro: 7th Street/Metro Center

Patina £££ ④ This stunning New American restaurant, located in the Disney Concert Hall, serves up flawless dishes to an appreciative audience of concertgoers and elite city workers. It wouldn't seem out of place in Beverly Hills – the quality is that good. ⓐ 141 S Grand Avenue ⓣ (213) 972 3331 ⓦ www.patinagroup.com ⓛ On non-performance days at the Concert Hall: 11.30–13.30, 17.00–21.30 Tues–Fri, 17.00–21.30 Sat, 16.00–21.30 Sun; on performance days: 11.30–13.30, 17.00–23.00 Tues–Fri, 17.00–23.00 Sat, 16.00–23.00 Sun ⓝ Metro: Civic Center; Bus: 2, 4, 10, 14, 714

BARS & CLUBS
Roof at The Standard When this place first opened, it was crawling with celebs and their hangers-on. It's not as cool as it used to be, but it still offers plenty of opportunities to play with the elite of LA. ⓐ The Standard Downtown Hotel, 550 S Flower Street ⓣ (213) 892 8080 ⓦ www.standardhotels.com ⓛ 12.00–01.30 ⓝ Metro: 7th Street; Bus: 16

CINEMAS & THEATRES
Dorothy Chandler Pavilion Part of the Music Centre of Los Angeles County, this space is no longer the prime classical music venue it once was, but it still plays host to the LA Opera. Most visitors will, however, know it as the venue that hosted the Academy Awards until the construction of the Kodak Theatre in Hollywood.

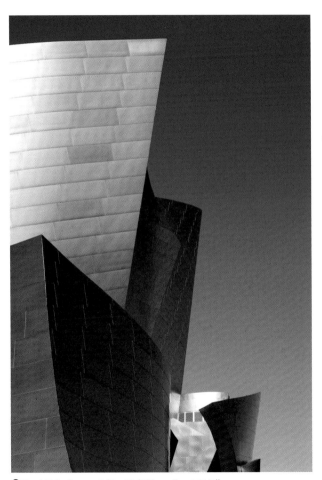

◯ *Frank Gehry's eye-catching Walt Disney Concert Hall*

ⓐ 135 N Grand Avenue ⓣ (213) 972 7211 ⓦ www.musiccenter.org
ⓛ Box office: 10.00–18.00 Mon–Sat ⓜ Metro: Civic Center;
Bus: 2, 4, 10, 14

Music Center of Los Angeles County This massive performing
arts centre has two large stages in the form of the 2,000-seat
Ahmanson Theater and the 739-seat Mark Taper Forum along
with the smaller 317-seat Kirk Douglas Theatre. The complex
also includes the Dorothy Chandler Pavilion and the Walt Disney
Concert Hall. Big touring productions and Broadway plays
constitute the bulk of the offerings on the two main stages.
Other performance spaces dotted around the complex house
smaller, more challenging work. ⓐ 135 N Grand Avenue
ⓣ (213) 628 2772 or (213) 972 0711 ⓦ www.centertheatregroup.org
ⓛ Box office: 12.00–18.00 Mon–Fri, 11.00–17.00 Sat & Sun, and
two hours prior to all performances ⓜ Metro: Civic Center;
Bus: 2, 4, 10, 14

Walt Disney Concert Hall This performance venue dedicated
to classical music opened to rave reviews in 2003. Designed
by Frank Gehry, it offers almost perfect acoustics and is now
home to the celebrated LA Philharmonic. ⓐ 111 S Grand Avenue
ⓣ (213) 972 7211 ⓦ www.laphil.org ⓛ Box office: 12.00–18.00
Tues–Sun ⓜ Metro: Civic Center; Bus: 2, 4, 10, 14

▶ *Picture perfect: Malibu beach at sunset*

Anaheim – the Heart of Orange County

Made famous by the teenage soap opera, *The O.C.*, Orange County is a land of wealth and privilege where the rich frolic and the poor don't exist. Golden sun drips on the shores of this hugely wealthy county – once home to arch-Republican president, Richard Nixon.

More famous than the kids of *The O.C.* is the inland community of Anaheim. A suburban town if ever there was one, there wouldn't be much to warrant going out of your way to visit if it wasn't for the world's most famous amusement park, Disneyland®.

Most international visitors consider a stop at Disneyland® a 'must do', with plenty choosing to avoid Los Angeles completely in favour of a holiday in this part of the state.

Anaheim is in contrast to Orange County's wealth and privilege, known for years as the home of Middle American values in a region of excess. Strip malls and cheap motels dot the area, drawn to its proximity to America's most well-known theme park, Disneyland®.

Walt Disney selected Anaheim as the site of his dream playground because of the acres of cheap land that surrounded it. At the time of completion, the entire area was clustered with orange groves – and not the tract housing that it currently holds. Orlando owes Anaheim a great debt for it is the success of this community that prompted Disney to create another park in a more rural area. Disney simply didn't want his dream distracted by concrete malls and high-rise hotels. Despite this, Disneyland® continues to charm millions every year. And where success blossoms, others follow – specifically in the form of the more ride-orientated Knott's Berry Farm. The basic rule of thumb is that younger kids and fans of childhood memories love Disneyland® while teens and thrill-seekers go to Knott's Berry Farm. The choice is yours.

Anaheim Tourist Office/Orange County Visitor & Convention Bureau ⓐ 800 W Katella Avenue ⓣ (714) 765 8888 ⓦ www.anaheimoc.org ⓛ 08.00–17.30 Mon–Fri

🔺 *Downtown Anaheim*

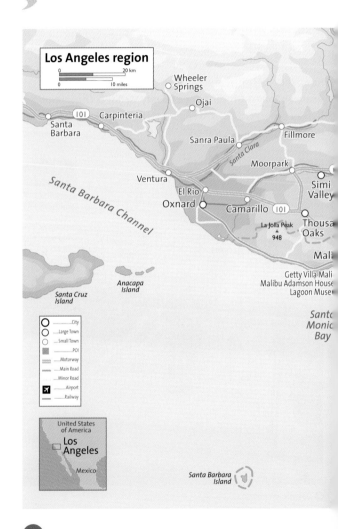

Los Angeles region

0 — 20 km
0 — 10 miles

Wheeler Springs

Ojai

Carpinteria

Santa Barbara

Sanra Paula

Fillmore

Santa Clara

Moorpark

Ventura

El Rio

Oxnard

Camarillo

Simi Valley

La Jolla Peak
948

Thousa Oaks

Mal

Santa Barbara Channel

Getty Villa Mali
Malibu Adamson House
Lagoon Muse

Anacapa Island

Santa Cruz Island

Santa Monic Bay

○ ....City
○ ....Large Town
○ ....Small Town
▪ ....POI
........Motorway
........Main Road
........Minor Road
✈ ....Airport
........Railway

United States of America

Los Angeles

Mexico

Santa Barbara Island

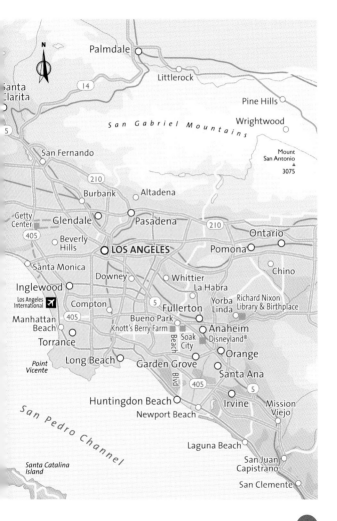

GETTING THERE

Interstate 5, otherwise known as the Santa Ana Freeway, will take you directly to Anaheim from Los Angeles. In the event that it is busy, take Interstate 405 (the San Diego Freeway) until you reach Highway 22 (the Garden Grove Freeway) and follow the signs. For Knott's Berry Farm, take Interstate 5 and exit at Beach Boulevard heading south.

SIGHTS & ATTRACTIONS

Disneyland®

Dubbed 'the happiest place on earth', Disneyland® is a world unto itself. Two parks make up the actual resort: Disneyland® and Disney's California Adventure®, a salute to the sights and icons of the great state. If the kid-orientated rides and shows get too much, there's even an adult-focused strip of bars and restaurants (including a branch of the House of Blues) at Downtown Disney®, just outside the main park.

Disneyland® Park

The Disneyland® complex is divided into various lands, each with a different theme. If you've been to a Disneyland® anywhere, the parks follow the same concept. Main Street USA acts as the central street from which all the lands spoke out. Almost Norman Rockwell-esque in appearance, it's a salute to an America of yesteryear complete with barbershop quartets and a clanging trolley. Going clockwise from the entrance, the first land you will encounter is Adventureland, which hosts

RICHARD NIXON LIBRARY & BIRTHPLACE

Nixon may have been a controversial figure, but you'll get a better idea as to why the 37th President of the United States was so eager to succeed when you see the displays that chronicle his modest upbringing. Artefacts include a number of treasured gifts given to him by celebrities and dignitaries during his time in office. 📍 18001 Yorba Linda Boulevard, Yorba Linda 📞 (714) 993 3393 🌐 www.nixonlibraryfoundation.org 🕐 10.00–17.00 Mon–Sat, 11.00–17.00 Sun 🚍 Bus: OC26. Admission charge

attractions like Indiana Jones and the Jungle Cruise. Next up is New Orleans Square. Here you will find the Pirates of the Caribbean ride that spawned the massive film trilogy. Lying beyond this and the Haunted Mansion is Critter Country. Strictly for the kids, it's the home of Winnie the Pooh and Br'er Rabbit. Continue clockwise to reach Frontierland, a rough-and-tumble zone that salutes America's early settlers. Directly opposite the park's main gates, at the end of Main Street USA, is Fantasyland. Then there is Tomorrowland – home to the wildest ride in the park, Space Mountain. As technology changes so fast, this zone can feel decidedly dated, but the kitschy 'Jetsons' feel adds something to the charm of the place. Between Fantastyland and Tomorrowland, is Mickey's Toontown, with the houses of its namesake resident and all of his friends. If you're looking for Mickey, he'll likely either be hanging out here, or in Town

Square, at the opposite end of Main Street from Fantasyland.
1313 S Harbor Boulevard (714) 781 4000 www.disneyland.com
Hours vary so check website before you visit Bus: OC205, OC430. Admission charge

Disney's California Adventure®

The great state of California is honoured in this theme park that lies over the former Disneyland® car park. While it isn't as big or as engrossing, the park has a number of benefits, including wilder rides and the opportunity to drink alcohol. If you've already been to Santa Monica, you may notice a similar flavouring to the look and feel of the place, as many of the rides and attractions were based on the Santa Monica pier. Highlights include the flight simulator called Soarin' Over California and the largest roller-coaster ever built in a Disney theme park, California Screamin.
1313 S Harbor Boulevard (714) 781 4000 www.disneyland.com
Hours vary so check website before you visit Bus: OC205, OC430. Admission charge

Knott's Berry Farm

Some may say that Knott's Berry Farm is like a poor man's version of Disneyland®, but they would be missing the point. Years ago, this plot of land was used to sell the homemade preserves of the Knott family that lived onsite. While the farm is no longer, the preserves are still here, along with a heavily nostalgic feeling that gives Main Street USA a run for its money. You may want to avoid trying the eateries and the 'down-home' country fare that is served all over the park until after you attempt the massive parachute drop and roller-coaster. Rides here are a lot more challenging

○ *Ride the Silver Bullet roller-coaster at Knott's Berry Farm*

than the comparably tame ones in Disneyland®. A large water park called **Soak City USA** ( 10.00–19.00 May–Oct) lies next door and features dozens of slides and a lazy river – perfect on hot summer days when you want to cool down.  8039 Beach Boulevard, Buena Park  (714) 220 5200  www.knotts.com  Hours vary so check website before you visit  Bus: OC29. Admission charge

TAKING A BREAK & AFTER DARK

Disneyland® offers plenty of eating options for all budgets; however, you will often find that even the cheapest bites and locales are overpriced and lacking in atmosphere. Two options that consistently rank top of the pile are the Cajun-inspired Blue Bayou in Disneyland® and the Italian alfresco eatery, the Golden Vine Terrace at Disney's California Adventure®. Opening hours for both establishments match those of the parks. Reservations can only be made through the park's main phone line.

El Misti Picanteria Arequipeña £–££ You might not be instantly drawn to the idea of Peruvian cuisine, but you'd be missing a good thing if you passed this dining spot. Hearty, authentic Incan dishes are on the menu. Good for a filling, intriguing meal.  3070 W Lincoln Avenue  (714) 995 5944  www.elmisticuisine.com  11.00–21.00 Tues–Sun  Bus: OC29, OC42

Catal Restaurant & Uva Bar ££ Probably the best dining option in Downtown Disney®, this Mediterranean bar and restaurant serves tapas – so you can eat as much or as little as you want. Fine dining is located upstairs. The bar is below. Reservations are recommended if you want to go to the restaurant section. 1580 Disneyland Drive (714) 774 4442 www.patinagroup.com/catal Hours vary so check website before you visit Bus: 460, OC205, OC430

Napa Rose £££ It may be set inside a Disney-owned hotel, but this restaurant is considered the best in town. The wine list is full of local vintages to match the Californian cuisine on offer. Grand Californian Hotel, 1600 S Disneyland Drive (714) 300 7170 17.30–22.00 Bus: 460, OC205, OC430

ACCOMMODATION

Candy Cane Inn £users£ This delightful motel is surrounded by beautiful gardens and is a whole lot cheaper than the Disney-owned properties inside the park. Rooms combine 1950s kitsch with bright florals, and it's just a three-minute walk from the Disney main gate. A shuttle runs every half-hour free of charge for guests. 1747 S Harbor Boulevard (714) 774 5284 www.candycaneinn.net Bus: OC205, OC430

Portofino Inn £users£ Great value, all-suites hotel just across from Disneyland®. Rooms are spacious and simply furnished. A wonderful option for travelling families. It may not offer the quaintness of the Candy Cane or the convenience of the Disney properties, but it's certainly a lot cheaper. 1831 S Harbor Boulevard (714) 782 7600 www.portofinoinnanaheim.com Bus: OC205, OC430

Disneyland® Hotel £££ Disney's first hotel has been through a renovation to give the rooms a fresher feel. The pool is first-rate, and pleases the kids once they've tired of the park itself. A Disney theme is highlighted throughout the property, so be sure you like mice if you want any sleep. ⓐ 1150 W Magic Way ⓣ (714) 520 5005 ⓦ www.disney.com ⓝ Bus: OC205, OC430

Disney's Grand Californian Hotel £££ Inspired by the architecture of Frank Lloyd Wright, this stunning hotel is a luxurious tribute to the craftsmanship of California. Roaring fireplaces will keep you toasty warm during the winter months. Kids will love the child-friendly touches, such as sleeping bags and bunk beds. You even benefit from a queueless private entrance to Disney's California Adventure®. ⓐ 1600 S Disneyland Drive ⓣ (714) 635 2300 ⓦ www.disney.com ⓝ Bus: OC205

Disney's Paradise Pier Hotel £££ Considered the budget option of the Disney hotels, it's far from cheap, with a room starting at, on average, $250 per night. A beach theme pervades the hotel, complete with a cute boardwalk. Take advantage of the early access to the parks and discounted tickets only offered to Disney hotel guests to make your dollars stretch even further. ⓐ 1717 Disneyland Drive ⓣ (714) 999 0990 ⓦ www.disney.com ⓝ Bus: OC205, OC430

Malibu & the coast

Although the area to the west of Los Angeles is dominated by the city of Malibu and its A-list-celeb associations, it is also a region of simple coastal resorts and stunning natural beauty.

MALIBU

While Beverly Hills, Brentwood and Bel Air are known as pricey neighbourhoods, Malibu is the pick of the bunch. The city of Malibu is actually a thin strip of land caught between the Santa Monica Mountains and the Pacific Ocean, with 43 km (27 miles) of the Pacific Coast Highway running right down the middle along the coast. Celebrities flock here to enjoy their privacy, yet a little-known law dictates that every speck of oceanside sand is public property – so if you know where a star lives, you have every chance of spotting them in their back garden if you walk along the beach. Locals fight hard to battle against the regular floods and fires that consume the area, and when you see how pristine the region is, you'll understand why. Pamela Anderson, David Geffen, Barbra Streisand, Tom Hanks and Courteney Cox-Arquette are just some of the big names who call Malibu home.
Malibu Chamber of Commerce ⓐ Suite 210, 23805 Stuart Ranch Road ⓣ (310) 456 9025 ⓦ www.malibu.org ⓝ None; instead, take Interstate 10 to the Pacific Coast Highway north exit

GETTING THERE
Follow Highway 1, the Pacific Coast Highway, straight to Malibu. But be warned, the traffic can be horrible at weekends, and

Friday evenings are when most of Los Angeles is trying to get out of town so it can be extremely busy then too.

SIGHTS & ATTRACTIONS
Getty Villa Malibu

Opened in 1974 as a venue to display oil billionaire J Paul Getty's extensive collection of Graeco-Roman antiquities, this structure is actually a copy of the Villa dei Papiri in Herculaneum. Critics found the holdings lacklustre, but the sheer folly of the architecture kept visitors coming back for more.

In 1997, most of the collection was moved to the Getty Center in Brentwood in order to pad out the exhibits of that

MALIBU ADAMSON HOUSE & LAGOON MUSEUM

Built just before the Great Depression, this magnificent home is a masterpiece of Colonial-style architecture. Take note of the colourful ceramic tiles – originally fired in a nearby pottery owned by the Rindge family that built the place. Next door is the Lagoon Museum, a historical museum that chronicles Malibu's past, from its early days as an Indian colony to its modern day status as home to the rich and famous. The regular house tour only covers the interior of the home. Adamson House Garden Tours are only available every Friday of the month at 10.00 (the fee is $5 per person and includes a house tour). ⓐ 23200 Pacific Coast Highway ⓘ (310) 456 8432 ⓦ www.adamsonhouse.org ⓛ 11.00–14.00 Wed–Sat ⓝ Bus: 434. Admission charge covers both sites

◒ *Enjoy the views from Pacific Coast Highway*

You can't get more Californian than when you're 'surfin' USA'

newer museum, forcing the villa to close for renovation. 2006
saw the reopening of the museum to great acclaim. Walls were
repainted, mosaics re-laid and new paths installed, all overlooked
by a large statue of Hercules. ⓐ 17985 Pacific Coast Highway
ⓣ (310) 440 7300 ⓦ www.getty.edu ⓛ 10.00–17.00 Thur–Mon
(bookings required) ⓝ Bus: 534

TAKING A BREAK & AFTER DARK

Neptune's Net £ A roadside seafood shack that's been a coastal
landmark since 1958 and regularly hosts a motley mix of surfers,
bikers, families and tourists. It's considered a great spot to pop
open a beer and enjoy the bounty of the ocean. ⓐ 42505 Pacific
Coast Highway ⓣ (310) 457 3095 ⓦ www.neptunesnet.com
ⓛ 10.30–20.00 Mon–Thur, 10.30–20.30 Fri, 10.00–20.30 Sat
& Sun ⓝ Bus: 534

Moonshadows £–££ Fresh fish caught daily is what's on
offer a this hip eatery that comes complete with a resident
weekend DJ. Due to the youthful vibe, a younger set patronises
this establishment, but that doesn't mean there is any lack
of quality. ⓐ 20356 Pacific Coast Highway ⓣ (310) 456 3010
ⓦ www.moonshadowsmalibu.com ⓛ Restaurant: 11.30–22.30
Mon–Thur, 11.30–23.00 Fri, 11.00–23.00 Sat, 11.00–22.00 Sun;
Blue Lounge bar: 11.30–00.00 Mon–Thur, 11.30–01.30 Fri,
11.00–01.30 Sat, 11.00–00.00 Sun ⓝ Bus: 534

Geoffrey's £££ Casual chic is what's served up at this restaurant
specialising in Californian cuisine. The dining room is actually
a cliffside deck providing stellar views of the ocean below.

Choose your vintage from an extensive wine list and sit back to soak up the relaxed atmosphere. ⓐ 27400 Pacific Coast Highway ⓣ (310) 457 1519 ⓦ www.geoffreysmalibu.com ⓛ 11.30–20.00 Mon–Thur, 11.30–23.00 Fri, 10.00–23.00 Sat, 10.00–22.00 Sun ⓝ Bus: 534

Nobu £££ This celebrity favourite is the original branch of the exclusive sushi restaurant that has taken over the world. The fish is so fresh it's practically swimming – but it's the Latin fusion of chillis and spices that keep them coming back for more. Book at least a month in advance or be prepared to eat at the bar. ⓐ 3835 Cross Creek Road ⓣ (310) 317 9140 ⓦ www.noburestaurants.com ⓛ 17.45–22.00 Sun–Thur, 17.45–23.00 Fri & Sat ⓝ Bus: 534

ACCOMMODATION

Casa Malibu Inn on the Beach ££–£££ Claiming to be a motel (but like no Travelodge you've ever seen), this intimate property is designed to resemble a friend's beach-house, complete with whirlpools, fireplaces and private decks. Stars such as Lana Turner and Robert De Niro have been known to frequent the place in times past when they needed a little down time. ⓐ 22752 Pacific Coast Highway ⓣ (310) 456 2219 ⓝ Bus: 534

Malibu Beach Inn £££ Multimillionaire film, theatre and record producer David Geffen owns this oceanfront hotel with a Spanish feel. A lobby bar and 24-hour room service will make you feel right at home. Be sure not to miss the delicious complimentary continental breakfast and afternoon tea session. ⓐ 22878 Pacific Coast Highway ⓣ (310) 456 6444 ⓦ www.malibubeachinn.com ⓝ Bus: 534

OJAI

Feeling a little hippy-dippy? Are your crystals out of alignment? Then head over to Ojai, where you can get your aura cleansed and enjoy a psychic reading without having to go to northern California. Ojai is SoCal's version of the Haight–Ashbury district, and is where Angelenos go when they need to feel spiritually centred. If you like whale song and panpipe music, then you've come to the right place. There's nothing specific to see or do in Ojai, rather, it's the collection of intriguing boutiques and galleries that line Ojai Avenue that make this a pleasant stop when going north from Los Angeles.

Ojai Visitors Bureau ⓐ 150 W Ojai Avenue ⓣ (805) 646 8126 ⓦ www.ojaichamber.org ⓛ 09.00–12.00, 13.00–16.00 Mon–Fri

GETTING THERE
Take the Pacific Coast Highway until you reach Ventura and then drive 19 km (12 miles) north out of town to Ojai.

TAKING A BREAK & AFTER DARK
Suzanne's Cuisine £–££ Café-style cuisine that's good for a light lunch or a more intimate meal. French touches abound on the menu, but it isn't all rich sauces and flavours. ⓐ 502 Ojai Avenue ⓣ (805) 640 1961 ⓦ www.suzannescuisine.com ⓛ 11.30–14.30, 18.00–22.30 Mon & Wed–Sun

Ranch House £££ Locals consider this Californian restaurant the finest in town. It's a bit of a drive from the centre of town, but worth every drop of fuel it takes to get there. ⓐ S Lomita

Avenue 🕿 (805) 646 2360 🌐 www.theranchhouse.com
🕒 17.30–20.30 Tues–Fri, 11.00–19.30 Sun, Sat hours vary so
phone or check website

ACCOMMODATION

Blue Iguana ££ Less quirky, yet also less expensive than its sister
property, the Emerald Iguana (see below), the Blue Iguana is a
great place to rest your head. Just be sure to like country-style
furnishings or you may find it all a bit too twee. 🔾 11794 N Ventura
Avenue 🕿 (805) 646 5277 🌐 www.blueiguanainn.com

Emerald Iguana ££–£££ Quaint cottages, each one given a
personal touch. Furnishings are on the Bohemian side, but
always comfortable. 🔾 108 Pauline Street 🕿 (805) 646 5277
🌐 www.emeraldiguana.com

SANTA BARBARA

Depending on when you travel, it can take anything from a few
hours to a full day to reach this popular, exclusive resort town
on the Pacific Coast Highway. Locals know they are on to a good
thing and like to keep the town looking ship-shape in order to
show off their wealth.

Santa Barbara differs from other coastal resort towns because
of its intriguing history and culture. The Spanish founded one of
their oldest missions in this region back in 1728 – a building that
can still be visited today. So ignore the associations Santa Barbara
has as the home of Michael Jackson's Neverland residence, because
that's about all the new money you're going to find here. Instead,

head to State Street for some café culture and boutique shopping. The price tags may leave you in shock but a spot of window shopping and a bit of people watching won't cost a cent.

Santa Barbara CVB ⓐ 1 Garden Street ⓣ (805) 966 9222 ⓦ www.sbchamber.org ⓛ 08.30–17.00 Mon–Fri

GETTING THERE

Follow the Pacific Coast Highway approximately 130 km (81 miles) out of Los Angeles until you reach Santa Barbara. Greyhound bus services can be taken from the city.

SIGHTS & ATTRACTIONS

Santa Barbara Mission

Dating back to 1870, this mission building is a replacement for the one founded by the Spanish in 1786. Today, it is considered one of the most beautiful in California and continues to operate as a Catholic church. ⓐ 2201 Laguna Street ⓣ (805) 682 4713 ⓦ www.saintbarbaraparish.org ⓛ Vary but services every Sunday at 07.30, 09.00, 10.30, 12.00

TAKING A BREAK & AFTER DARK

Brophy Bros £–££ Pick up a bowl of this establishment's famous clam chowder and you'll be sure to want to lick the bowl by the end of your meal. If soup isn't your thing, then the fresh fish will be. ⓐ 119 Harbor Way ⓣ (805) 966 4418 ⓦ www.brophybros.com ⓛ 10.00–22.00 Sun–Thur, 10.00–23.00 Fri & Sat

Da Dario £££ A popular upmarket Italian eatery that's numbered among the top restaurants in town by locals and visitors alike.

It's run by a native Italian who worked his way up through many popular SoCal eateries. The atmosphere is cosy and romantic. ⓐ 37 E Victoria Street ① (805) 884 9419 ⓦ www.cadario.net ① 11.30–14.00, 17.30–23.30 Mon–Sat, 17.30-22.30 Sun

ACCOMMODATION

Santa Barbara Tourist Hostel £ You might be surprised to find a hostel in a town as chic as this, but it's a great place for those who want to experience a bit of high living on a budget. ⓐ 134 Chapala Street ① (805) 963 0154 ⓦ www.sbhostel.com

Hotel Santa Barbara ££–£££ A great property if you want convenience combined with comfort. The beach is a short, five-minute walk away. ⓐ 533 State Street ① (800) 549 9869 ⓦ www.hotelsantabarbara.com

Biltmore – Four Seasons £££ Dripping with gold gilt, marble and plush, soft furnishings, this hotel is a temple to comfort – and located right next to the prettiest cove in town. Definitely worth the money. ⓐ 1260 Channel Drive ① (805) 969 2261 ⓦ www.fourseasons.com

---

▶ *Stretch Hummers – fun, but not so practical for getting around*

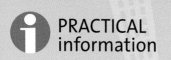

PRACTICAL
information

Directory

GETTING THERE

By air

The only international gateway serving airlines from Europe and beyond is Los Angeles International Airport, otherwise known as LAX. Other airports exist in Santa Monica and Burbank, but serve only short-haul routes. LAX is not known for its friendliness or efficiency, so try to avoid spending too much time here if at all possible. Depending on traffic and where you are going to, a taxi

⬣ *The landmark sky bar at LAX*

from LAX will cost $25 plus tip for the Westside or double that
for destinations in Hollywood, Beverly Hills or Santa Monica.
A flat rate of $42 exists for rides to Downtown. A surcharge of
$2.50 is added for every taxi fare from LAX. Those on a budget
can attempt public transport – but you will need both time
and patience to make it work. Take either the C or G shuttle
bus to Aviation Blvd station on the MetroRail Green Line and
then sit down for a long ride. A better option is to book a ride
on SuperShuttle, a shared-ride service that will drop you off
at your hotel, starting from $25. Shuttles are available outside
the arrivals terminals (see page 50).

Many people are aware that air travel emits CO_2, which
contributes to climate change. You may be interested in the
possibility of lessening the environmental impact of your flight
through the charity **Climate Care** (ⓦ www.climatecare.org),
which offsets your CO_2 by funding environmental projects
around the world.

By rail

Though travelling by rail is often a more expensive option than
domestic flying in the USA, it at least allows you the chance to
see something of America's great Western countryside en route.
All train journeys depart and arrive at Los Angeles' glorious
Union Station, located at 800 N Alameda Street in Downtown.

Amtrak is the only company offering passenger train services
in the United States. Lines run along the Pacific Coast or cross-
country, depending on how much of the country you want to
see and which corners you are coming from.

Amtrak reservations ⓣ 001 800 872 7245 ⓦ www.amtrak.com

By road

The highway system in southern California is extremely well integrated into the American Interstate system. In fact, it is claimed that a notorious case of collusion among the big American automobile manufacturers destroyed the city's once-famous public transport system in order to force residents to buy more cars.

The result is a spider's web of highways that can whisk visitors to almost every corner of the city. Unfortunately, it also results in regular traffic snarls and cases of road rage. Don't be put off by the negative press, as extreme incidents are few – just be sure to check your maps before you get on the road in order to ensure that you know where you are going in advance.

Long-distance buses connect Los Angeles with most other North American cities. Travel costs can often be expensive, so be sure to check prices in advance. Bookings can be made on ① (800) 231 2222 or ⓦ www.greyhound.com

The main bus station is located at 1716 East 7th Street in Downtown. ① Be warned, this is not a pleasant neighbourhood, so be aware of your surroundings at all times.

ENTRY FORMALITIES

Visitors to the United States who are citizens of countries under the Visa Waiver Scheme, such as the UK, Ireland, Australia and New Zealand, will need a machine-readable passport, but not a visa, for stays of 90 days or fewer. Canadians do not need visas, but will need a valid passport. Canadian birth certificates and driving licences will not be permitted as proof of ID following the implementation of new restrictions by the

American government.

Most personal effects and the following items are duty-free: 200 cigarettes or 50 cigars (not Cuban) or 2 kg ($4^{1}/_{2}$ lb) of smoking tobacco, 1 litre ($^{1}/_{4}$ gal) of wines or spirits (over 21), up to $100 in gifts and $10,000 in cash, traveller's cheques or endorsed bank drafts.

As entry requirements and customs regulations are subject to change, you should always check the current situation with your local travel agent, airline or an American embassy or consulate before you leave. You can double-check entry requirements at ⓦ http://travel.state.gov or ⓦ www.usembassy.org.uk before your scheduled departure.

MONEY

The currency in the United States is the US dollar. A dollar is divided into 100 cents. Currency denominations are: 100 dollars, 50 dollars, 20 dollars, 10 dollars, 5 dollars, 1 dollar, 25 cents (quarter), 10 cents (dime), 5 cents (nickel), 1 cent (penny). There are also 50 cent and 1 dollar coins, but these are used infrequently.

You can withdraw cash from ATMs at almost all American banks. Credit cards are widely accepted for almost all transactions, with Visa, MasterCard and American Express being the most common forms of plastic.

HEALTH, SAFETY & CRIME

It is not necessary to take any special health precautions while travelling in the United States. Tap water is safe to drink, but many locals prefer to drink the bottled varieties.

Pharmacies (or drug stores) are located throughout the city – many offering extended hours in accordance with American demands. American pharmacists are extremely well informed. Many drugs distributed over-the-counter in Europe will need a doctor's prescription in the United States, due to tougher restrictions placed by the FDA (Food and Drug Administration). Be sure to bring prescriptions with you if you require any form of medication during your travels.

American healthcare is of an excellent standard, but it is extremely expensive. A minor ailment requiring an overnight stay could result in expenses of thousands of dollars. As such, be sure to take out travel insurance prior to departure.

As in many other big cities, crime is a fact of life in Los Angeles. Most cases of violent crime are restricted to neighbourhoods you will most likely not be visiting during your stay. One exception being Downtown, which is fine during daylight hours in the week, but can get decidedly unwelcoming after dark and at weekends.

When using public transport or walking on the street, carry your wallet in your front pocket, keep bags closed at all times, never leave valuables on the ground when you are seated at a table and always wear camera bags and purses crossed over your chest. Also, be sure to place all purchases in the boot of your car and lock the doors whenever you park it – even if you're just popping into a shop for a few seconds. For details of emergency numbers, see page 138.

OPENING HOURS

Most businesses open Monday–Friday 10.00–18.00. Shopping centres always stay open later, until about 21.00.

Cultural institutions are usually open from 09.00–18.00, though extended hours are possible on selected days during the week.

Late night openings and the concept of staying open '24 hours' started in the Los Angeles area, so don't be surprised if you see boutiques and restaurants open even into the wee hours of the morning.

TOILETS

As almost everyone drives in Los Angeles, the concept of public toilets is largely unknown. Instead, locals make use of the public facilities at the numerous shopping centres that are scattered throughout the city. Restaurants, bars and hotels tend not to have too much of a problem if you use their facilities. Also, petrol stations are a common place for relief for drivers. Don't be surprised if the key is attached to a massive brick or concrete block – this is how they prevent it from wandering.

CHILDREN

Los Angeles is generally a child-friendly place and no special health precautions need be taken for children. While the proliferation of cars and long distances prevents kids from playing on the streets or heading to a local park, there are still plenty of activities to keep the tots occupied.

Nappies and other baby articles can be readily obtained from supermarkets and drug stores. Things to see and do with the kids while in town include:

Farmers' Market Fussy eaters will love this colourful market stocked with the best fare the city has on offer. Choose from staples such as pizza and burgers or experiment with more regional cuisine. Follow it up with a ride on the mini-train at

the adjoining Grove shopping centre (see page 69) for a full afternoon of fun. ⓐ Corner of West 3rd Street and S Fairfax Avenue ⓦ www.farmersmarketla.com ⓛ 09.00–21.00 Mon–Fri, 09.00–20.00 Sat, 10.00–19.00 Sun ⓝ Bus: 16, 217

Griffith Park Let them run freely in the city's favourite green space. Live music often adds to the fun. Choose from a 1920s carousel, horse rides or a petting zoo to fill the hours. There's even an observatory that's great for kids who like seeing stars – and not of the celebrity kind. ⓐ 4700 Western Heritage Way ⓣ (323) 913 4688 ⓛ 05.00–22.00

COMMUNICATIONS
Internet

Internet access is provided by most hotels and in branches of the LA Public Library System. Those with laptops can also take advantage of the free wireless hotspots that have been set up in parts of Long Beach, Culver City, Hermosa Beach and Pershing Square in Downtown.

Phone

Coin-operated public phones are common throughout the city – but all have different suppliers, so you will not find that there is a standard appearance for phone booths. Local calls cost 50¢, with charges increasing according to distance and length of call. Be sure to have plenty of change on hand. A recorded voice will inform you when you need to add funds. For international calls from a payphone, have a credit card ready and try to find a machine that allows you to swipe your card – otherwise you'll have to be ready with more small change than the average cash machine.

TELEPHONING THE US

For dialling into Los Angeles, use the US country code (001) plus the local area code followed by the seven-digit number. Local area codes are as follows:

213: Downtown

310: Malibu, Santa Monica, Venice Beach, Culver City, West LA, Westwood, Beverly Hills, sections of West Hollywood, Inglewood

323: Sections of West Hollywood, Hollywood, East LA, South Central

562: Long Beach

626: San Gabriel Valley

818: San Fernando Valley

949: Laguna and Newport Beaches

714: Orange County

805: San Luis Obispo, Santa Barbara, Ventura

TELEPHONING ABROAD

When making an international call, dial the international code you require and drop the initial zero of the area code you are ringing. The international dialling code for calls from the United States to Australia is 011 61, to the UK 011 44, to the Irish Republic 011 353, to South Africa 011 27, and to New Zealand 011 64. Calls to Canada from the United States do not require an international dialling code.

Post

Postal services are quick and efficient. Stamps can be bought at post offices or from most drug stores. Post boxes are blue. Postcards within the US cost 27¢ or 70¢ to Europe.

ELECTRICITY

The standard electrical current is 110–120 V. Two-pin adaptors can be purchased at most electrical shops.

TRAVELLERS WITH DISABILITIES

Facilities for visitors with disabilities are generally quite good in the United States. These facilities are usually indicated by a blue pictogram of a person in a wheelchair. Strict building codes ensure there are reserved car parks for people in wheelchairs, and motorised service stops, airports and main railway stations always have suitable toilet facilities. Special 'lift' buses are available for visitors in wheelchairs.

Facilities for visitors with disabilities arriving at the city's main international airports are good, though travellers with special needs should inform their airlines in advance.

A useful source of advice when in California is the **Society for the Advancement of Travel for the Handicapped** ℹ (212) 447 7284 🕸 www.sath.org

TOURIST INFORMATION

The main branch of the tourist office is located Downtown. The office is an excellent source for both maps and information. **Los Angeles Convention & Visitors Bureau** ⓐ 685 S Figueroa Street at Wilshire Boulevard ℹ (213) 689 8822 🕸 www.lacvb.com

🕐 08.30–17.00 Mon–Fri Ⓜ Metro: 7th Street/Metro Center;
Bus: 60, 760, 20

BACKGROUND READING

The Black Dahlia, L.A. Confidential by James Ellroy. The master
of modern Hollywood noir.
Hollywood Babylon by Kenneth Anger. The dark side of the
industry of dreams.
Translating LA by Paul Theroux. Uncover the neighbourhoods
of Los Angeles with one of the masters of the genre.

Emergencies

EMERGENCY NUMBERS
Ambulance, Fire Brigade, Police  911

MEDICAL SERVICES
While healthcare is excellent in Southern California, it doesn't come cheap. Make sure that you have private travel insurance. For serious emergencies, go directly to the emergency departments of the main public hospitals.

Emergency pharmacy
Pharmacies are located throughout the city and many are open 24 hours. Prescription and non-prescription drugs (including aspirin) are only sold at pharmacies.

Hospitals
Cedars-Sinai Medical Center 8700 Beverly Boulevard at George Burns Road, West Hollywood (310) 423 3277 www.csmc.edu Bus: 14
Century City Doctors' Hospital 2070 Century Park East, between Constellation and Olympic Boulevards, Century City (310) 772 4000 www.ccdoctorshospital.com Bus: 28, 728
St John's Health Center 1328 22nd Street at Santa Monica Boulevard, Santa Monica (310) 829 5511 www.stjohns.org Bus: 4, 704

POLICE

In the event that you require police assistance, dial 911 to be put through to the pertinent contact.

Lost property

If you lose anything or suspect that it has been stolen, contact the police. While an officer is with you, you will need to make a statement and fill in the required forms for insurance purposes.

For items lost at LAX, try your airline, followed by the lost property number on ❶ (310) 417 0440. Items lost on MTA buses or trains can be traced through ❶ (323) 937 8920.

EMBASSIES & CONSULATES

Australian Consulate ⓐ 2029 Century Park East at W Olympic Boulevard, West LA ❶ (310) 229 4800

British Consulate ⓐ 11766 Wilshire Boulevard at A Carmelina Avenue, West LA ❶ (310) 481 0031

Canadian Consulate ⓐ 550 S Hope Street, between West 5th & West 6th Streets, Downtown ❶ (213) 346 2700

Irish Consulate ⓐ 751 Seadrift Drive, Huntington Beach ❶ (714) 658 9832

New Zealand Consulate ⓐ 2425 Olympic Boulevard, Santa Monica ❶ (310) 566 6555

Editorial/project management: Lisa Plumridge
Copy editor: Paul Hines
Layout/DTP: Alison Rayner

The publishers would like to thank the following individuals and organisations for supplying their copyright photographs for this book: Brian Boulos, page 73; Dreamstime.com (kineticimagery, page 105; Gary Lewis, page 30; Ken Wood, page 81); Jose Gil/BigStockPhoto.com, page 113; Pictures Colour Library, page 26; James Quine/Alamy, page 11; Konrad Summers, page 51; Martijn de Visse, page 107; World Pictures, pages 17 & 34–5; Rob Young, page 74; Mark Bassett/The Source, all others.

Send your thoughts to
books@thomascook.com

- **Found a great bar, club, shop or must-see sight that we don't feature?**
- **Like to tip us off about any information that needs a little updating?**
- **Want to tell us what you love about this handy little guidebook and more importantly how we can make it even handier?**

Then here's your chance to tell all! Send us ideas, discoveries and recommendations today and then look out for your valuable input in the next edition of this title.

Email the above address (stating the title) or write to: CitySpots Series Editor, Thomas Cook Publishing, PO Box 227, Coningsby Road, Peterborough PE3 8SB, UK.